THE
ARMS PARK

heart of a rugby nation

Bill O'Keefe & Emyr Young

*This book is dedicated to those who care
about the great heritage of our national game*

First impression: 2012

The publishers wish to acknowledge the support of
Cyngor Llyfrau Cymru

Design: Y Lolfa
Cover photograph: Cardiff Library

Every attempt was made to ascertain
and contact the source of all the photographs in this book.

ISBN: 978 184771 353 7

FSC

Published and printed in Wales
on paper from well maintained forests
by Y Lolfa Cyf., Talybont, Ceredigion SY24 5HE
website www.ylolfa.com
e-mail ylolfa@ylolfa.com
tel 01970 832 304
fax 832 782

Foreword

When Bill O'Keefe and Emyr Young sent me the manuscript of this fascinating book, the first fact I read revealed that Wales's sporting citadel stands on the site of a Roman port. How appropriate. After all, the Romans knew a thing or two about successful stadiums. It wasn't enough to pack in 70,000 spectators, several unfortunate Christians, a few hungry lions and hope for instant atmosphere. The key was variety.

Those rugged Russell Crowe-types dispatched each other using a myriad of combat techniques. Before the gladiators got the thumbs-up or down, the crowd was treated to jugglers, acrobats, performing animals and music. If savage blood-letting wasn't your bag, you could always plump for some thrilling Ben Hur-style motor sport instead.

Cardiff has had its own coliseum for more than 130 years. And just as a Welsh rugby victory creates the same sort of frenzy as Maximus wielding his sword in 180 AD, it too has had more than one spectating experience. It has also enjoyed several incarnations from the acre of meadowland gifted to the city for recreational pursuits by the Third Marquess of Bute to the concrete cathedral where the gods of '70s rugby were worshipped.

For my generation, it's the Millennium Stadium that draws the faithful. Since its angled steel masts – the highest points in Cardiff – first pierced the horizon, it has established itself as a chameleon arena, changing its colours to suit a wide spectrum of events. When fans say "I Was There" they could be referring to anything from Mark Taylor scoring the stadium's first try to Nicky Wire in a fetching pink frock leading 60,000 revellers into a new century.

Design plays its part in creating such a versatile venue. When the Romans got too hot, they whipped a giant awning over the Coliseum to shade themselves. The Millennium Stadium's more hi-tech method of avoiding the elements – 8,000 tonnes of sliding metal roof – ensures the switch from outdoor to indoor arena can be done in twenty minutes for under a fiver. In the words of rugby's troubadour Max Boyce: "They slide it back when Wales attack so God can watch us play."

Since 1876 Welsh sport has also been beautifully located bang in the middle of town. Having sampled arenas from Marseilles to Melbourne, Dublin to Durban and Twickers to Ellis Park – trudging to the nether regions of cities all over the world – none can compete with the uniquely central location of our national stadium.

Yet ultimately, for all these positional benefits and architectural wonders, it's the people who make the difference. The Romans didn't get everything right – they banished women and plebs to the loftiest tiers. But the demographics of Welsh sporting crowds have always reflected the nation as a whole. Indeed the tradition of female support is as old as Welsh rugby itself. The first grandstand on the old Cardiff Arms Park was built in 1881 "for the convenience of the spectators and the ladies in particular".

The match days of the modern era are a family affair, young painted faces adding colour to the carnival. And the soundtrack still matters too. The stadiums have shaped the greatest choral tradition in sport. The Arms Park introduced the national anthem to rugby. In a cunning tactic to counter the psychological warfare of the Haka, the Welsh team that beat New Zealand in 1905 led the crowd in a rousing rendition of *Hen Wlad Fy Nhadau* for the first time ever. More than 100 years later the "gwlads" still bounce off the roof of the Millennium.

But of course those who perform on Wales's premier sporting stage have given us so much to sing about. The Arms Park has witnessed three glittering eras of Welsh rugby – the 1900s, the early '50s and the '70s. In its relatively short life, the Millennium's attractions have spanned the sublime skills of Rivaldo (Wales v Brazil) and the more esoteric appeal of the Home Nations Petanque Championship. Not to mention boxing, speedway, six FA Cup finals, four Heineken Cup finals and Rugby World Cups in both codes. And in 2012 it's where the Olympics begin. The opening event of the Games – the women's football – kicks off in Cardiff.

In all these communal experiences, we remember the personal moments. My father cherishes his Arms Park memories of Cliff Morgan's quicksilver skills helping Wales beat the All Blacks in 1953, the Empire Games bringing the world to Cardiff in 1958 and Gareth Edwards emerging from the red mud of the greyhound track with an instant face-pack in 1972 after scoring one of the most glorious tries the game has ever seen.

My nephew remembers his part in the closing ceremony of the 1999 Rugby World Cup, a Rhondda under-11s schoolboy rugby player carrying a corner of the Romanian flag. Now in his twenties, he still has the tuft of grass he snaffled as a souvenir that day.

And flicking through my own mental scrapbook of the Millennium, I realise it's given me some of the best days and nights of my life. I've watched a Beatle rock, the Stones roll and a boy who looked like Elvis kick Wales to victory over England with his golden boot.

I've cried tears of bliss as Martyn Williams launched the ball into a delirious crowd to signal Wales's first Grand Slam for 27 years and laughed with joy as they did it again just three years later. I've had moments of sheer terror too, once dangling from the stadium roof for a charity abseil. But landing safely on its hallowed turf, I looked up at the stands and had a fleeting taste of what it must be like for those who have danced and dazzled on this field of dreams by the side of the Taff.

This book contains their story. So to the generations of men and women who have brought our citadel of sport to life since 1876 – as the Romans would say – we salute you.

Carolyn Hitt

Introduction

Cardiff, or *Caerdydd* to give it its Welsh name, means the 'Fortress on the river Taff'. The name originates from almost 2,000 years ago when the invading forces of the Roman Empire constructed a military encampment on the site of what became Cardiff Castle, as they attempted to pacify the fierce local Celtic tribe, the Silures. Cardiff's Roman Fortress and its later Norman additions are still there, but to many modern Welsh people the real 'Fortress on the Taff' lies a couple of hundred yards to the west.

The Millennium Stadium now stands at the heart of Wales's capital city on a site known all over the rugby-playing world as the Cardiff Arms Park. Few sporting names are as closely linked to a nation's identity as that of the 'Arms Park' to Wales, and its position right at the centre of the capital reflects this relationship. First time visitors to Cardiff are often surprised to see what looks like a large space ship which has touched down in the city centre. Not many sports grounds are afforded the privilege of such a central position in a national capital, but this latter day coliseum is no ordinary sports ground.

The Millennium Stadium, the latest incarnation of the Arms Park, opened in 1999 in time for Wales to host the Rugby World Cup. It seats over 75,000 people, or to put it another way about 2.5 per cent of the population of Wales at one time, and when its retractable roof is closed it is Europe's largest indoor arena. It is a striking building and one which has already become synonymous with Wales. It is also one of the world's most versatile arenas, capable of hosting anything from rugby and football matches to rock concerts, speedway, rallying, cricket, boxing and many other events.

The story of this unique venue does not begin in 1999 however. It stretches back over 200 years and is closely connected to the story of Cardiff and Wales in that period. This book tells the remarkable story of this famous site, finishing with a look at the Millennium Stadium itself, regarded by many as the best in the world.

Bill O'Keefe and Emyr Young
February 2012

7

Chapter 1

In his book *A Pocket Guide: Cardiff* the eminent historian John Davies accurately describes Cardiff Arms Park as, "Wales's most renowned piece of real estate." Many would agree, but that was not always the case. For most of recorded history the site of the Arms Park was either in the waters of the river Taff or mired in the boggy tidal marshes beside it. The story of the ground is closely bound with that of the river, as we shall see.

The river Taff flows down from the Brecon Beacons to the sea at Cardiff, where a small port sprang into life with the arrival of the Romans. Visitors to the stadium have already unwittingly used the Roman port by crossing Westgate Street at the junction of Quay Street. The original course of the river was down present-day Westgate Street, so the stadium really stands on the west and not the east bank of the old river. Excavations in the 1970s revealed Roman trade at the site and that a small settlement had grown, protected by the Roman fort which later became Cardiff Castle. Later, Viking traders used it and left behind the name of the lane next to Quay Street, Womanby Street which should more correctly be Hundeman-By, meaning Huntsman's Dwelling. The original

quays were wooden but in the thirteenth century a stone quay, capable of handling larger vessels, was built for the increasing volume of shipping making its way up the Taff to trade at the little port.

The modest growth in shipping and prosperity created a new pastime for local people, namely piracy. To say that the denizens of Cardiff embraced piracy enthusiastically is a bit like saying that modern Welsh people are quite fond of rugby. In fact, until the advent of rugby, no activity seems to have united every strata of local society as much as piracy. Everyone seemed to be involved. Pirate crews were recruited, and drank, unloaded and sold their spoils and generally lived it up in the streets around the quay. Captured vessels would be moored up on the marshes under the present East Stand. In the 1500s the arrival of one of the better-known pirate crews would have been greeted with the enthusiasm and anticipation of a modern-day rugby international. It was not just ordinary towns folk who benefited from the pirates. The notorious Welsh pirate John Callys, described as 'the most dangerous pyrate in the Realm', had important connections in Cardiff. The Herbert Family (kinsmen of the Earls of Pembroke), controlled

The first Marquess of Bute was a Scots aristocrat who came into vast Welsh estates by marrying a local aristocrat, Charlotte Windsor, heiress of the Earls of Pembroke. In 1803 he designated a 'swampy meadow' by the Taff for recreation and so began the history of Cardiff Arms Park.

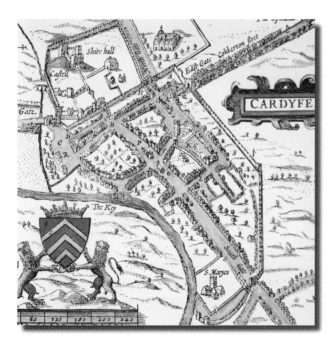

John Speed's 1610 Cardiff map shows the old course of the Taff and its meander towards the town quay. The site of the stadium then lay on the west bank where the shield is shown.

Cardiff and Nicholas Herbert was Callys's father-in-law. He also happened to be the Sheriff of Glamorgan and when in port, Callys lodged at his house. Thomas Lewis, Mayor of Cardiff, was one of Callys's customers, as was the Clerk to the Council of Wales and the Marches (in other words, the government!). No wonder a letter of 1577 complained, "Cardiff is the general resort of pyrates and there they are sheltered and protected."

The fun didn't stop with piracy either. The secluded wharfs and creeks of the Taff near the present-day stadium were also the centre of a thriving gun-running business by the enterprising and outwardly respectable Mathew family of Llandaff. During the 1580s, around 150 tons of ordnance from their Cardiff foundry was shipped to various destinations, including Spain. Spain happened to be threatening to invade Britain at the time, but that did not stand in the way of some good old-fashioned arms dealing.

The Taff like the rest of the south Wales coast was very tidal and prone to flooding. The worst instance came in January 1607 when what some experts believe was a tsunami swept up the Bristol Channel and overwhelmed the coast. The sea swept almost four miles (6.4km) inland, much faster than anyone could outrun it and, along the low lying coast around Cardiff and Newport, over 2,000 people drowned. The land where the

The Cardiff Arms Hotel, favoured Cardiff residence of the First Marquess of Bute, was demolished in 1878 and replaced by the grander Angel Hotel. Its name lived on in the nearby park created by the Butes. Originally called the Great Park, the nickname Cardiff Arms Park was adopted and stuck.

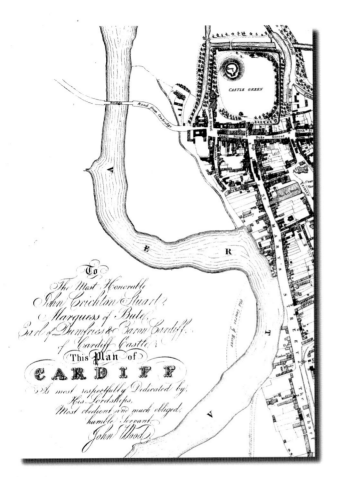

The Second Marquess of Bute began the development of Cardiff's docks in 1839. His insistence that Cardiff Arms park be kept for recreation is the reason the Millennium Stadium enjoys its wonderful central location.

stadium stands would have been under seawater for several weeks.

After repairs and rebuilding, Cardiff continued much as before. The town quay was the focus of trade and as before not all of it was strictly legal. With the suppression of piracy during the 18th century and the introduction of excise duties, the adaptable people on the banks of the Taff turned to smuggling. Two thousand pounds of tobacco was landed and seized near Cardiff in 1649 and this was the first recorded seizure of smuggled goods liable to excise duty. Everything that was subject to the duty was smuggled here: tea, soap, candles, brandy, rum, wine, tobacco, silk and even human hair for wig-making. The marshes, creeks and the tides of the area, together with convenient off-shore islands, such as Flat Holm, made it a smuggler's paradise. In addition, the extra cloak of secrecy

Mule trains with two-ton wagons were once the only way of moving coal and iron from the mountains of Glamorgan to the coast. The advent of the canal and railway transformed Cardiff from a sleepy coastal town to the world's busiest port.

provided by the Welsh language made catching and convicting the smugglers a hard task for the authorities. Local administrators and gentry were no help, as they were often the smugglers' best customers.

Into this cauldron of maritime skulduggery in the 1760s stepped a Scots nobleman, Lord Mountstuart. He had married Charlotte Windsor

Herbert, granddaughter of the Earl of Pembroke in 1766 and had inherited their estates, including much of Cardiff and the site of the Arms Park. He became the first Marquess of Bute in 1796 and although he did add to his Welsh estate, he spent little time here and disliked staying at the castle. As a result, he purchased the inn opposite, the Cardiff Arms Hotel, and used this as his base on

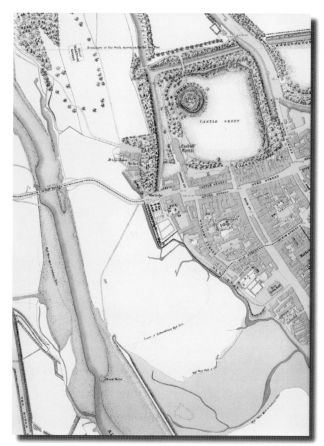

This 1851 map shown the growth of Cardiff and Brunel's work on the river diversion in progress. The brown shaded land is the old course that stubbornly refused to drain and was left as a boggy swamp until concerns over public health forced the Corporation to act in 1865.

The crowded courtyards along what became Westgate Street after the diversion contained some of the worst housing conditions in Britain. The overcrowding and lack of sanitation even shocked the Victorian health inspectors.

Welsh visits. The inn took its name from the coat of arms of Cardiff which he had received in 1776. It was a coaching inn and said to be the best in the town and it stood on the site of an earlier inn called the Red House which had burned down in 1770. The Red House was probably the Cardiff town home of the wealthy Morgan clan of Tredegar House and Ruperra Castle, relatives of Henry Morgan the buccaneer.

The location of the stadium and indeed Cardiff would have changed little over the last few centuries. In fact the first population census in 1801 stated that only 1,870 people lived there. This was probably not more than in the medieval times. In fact, a study of the burgage plots of the 1280s suggests a population of about 2,000. By the late 17th century the quay was in a poor state and the Taff was badly silted. The town's future prospects looked bleak. However this was all to change due to one commodity – coal. In 1782 a

Cardiff customs official stated, "We have no coal exported from this port, nor ever shall, as it would be too expensive to bring it down from the internal part of the country." It was probably not the greatest prediction the customs officer ever made, as, just over a century later, Cardiff was the world's greatest coal exporting port and was setting the global price of the world's fuel.

Iron from the new works at Merthyr Tydfil was already being shipped, but the only way of transporting it to Cardiff was by mule train or in two-ton horse drawn wagons. It was not economic to transport coal in this way and, as iron production increased rapidly. a solution was needed. The result was the Glamorgan Canal which opened in 1794 and connected Cardiff to its mineral-rich hinterland. A period of enormous change had begun and, although the growth was more steady than spectacular at first, the decision was made in the 1830s by the second Marquess of Bute to build Cardiff's first masonry dock. It opened in 1839 and within two years coal exports rose from 6,500 tons to nearly 87,000 tons per annum. This spelt the end for the old town quay and the small coastal town it once served. It was transforming itself into a major seaport.

The creation of the Arms Park was a by-product of this headlong rush in pursuit of prosperity.

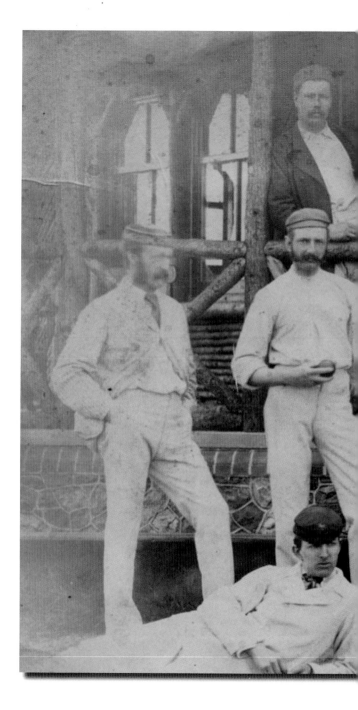

Cardiff Cricket Club was playing at the Arms Park by the late 1840s and the cricketers were instrumental in forming the rugby club as a way of continuing their association in the winter. This photo shows the fine Victorian gentlemen of Cardiff Cricket Club in 1875.

Cardiff's earliest team photograph and not a pirate in sight. Some early matches were played at Sophia Gardens, where this photo was taken, before a permanent move to the Arms Park.

The land between Canton Bridge and the old quay was designated for recreation by the Butes, and was known rather grandly as the Great Park. It was used for military displays, band concerts and, in 1837, was the site of a large firework display to mark the coronation of Queen Victoria. The first organised sport was played here in the 1840s but it was cricket, not rugby. Cardiff Cricket Club was founded in 1845 and was playing on the park in 1848. Cardiff Corporation had designs on the land for development and several schemes were put forward for discussion, most notably as a site for a cattle market but also for a new town hall and even a university. Two things saved the park: its tendency to flood which made it a less desirable plot, and the fact that the second Marquess insisted it remain for recreation. It is thanks to him, therefore, that the Millennium Stadium, Cardiff Arms Park is the most famous address in world rugby.

The flooding was a problem and the river Taff was seen as an impediment to growth, in particular to the arrival of the South Wales Railway (part of the Great Western Railway). They were keen to locate a station site close to the town centre. With the old town quay no longer used, there were no objections to the diversion of the Taff. The west to east meander towards the quay was straightened out by the GWR's famous engineer, Isambard

This salty sea-dog is wearing Cardiff RFC's first kit. In a short-lived nod to the town's piratical heritage, the club adopted the design until their Mams said 'no!'.

Isambard Kingdom Brunel demonstrating the term 'chain smoking' with a well-earned cigar. The chains in the photo were made at Pontypridd for *SS Great Britain*. Between 1849 and 1853 Brunel diverted the Taff to its present course and in so doing performed a great service to Welsh rugby by doubling the size of the Arms Park.

land now on the east bank of the Taff. However the land was no better than a swamp and neither the GWR or Cardiff Corporation could agree on who should pay to drain it. The riverbed was often filled with fetid water and with the massive growth in population crowded into courtyards and streets nearby, it presented a major health hazard. A cholera outbreak in the late 1840s claimed 383 lives and panic spread. Near to the present-day Westgate Street, there were a series of grim-looking courtyards packed with poor families, including many Irish immigrants escaping the famine. In 1850 T W Rammell, a Board of Health inspector described the scene as, "fearful, beyond anything of the kind I have ever known of". In one case 500 people lived in just 27 homes with only four toilets between them. In 1865 the corporation finally gave in and filled in the old riverbed. A new road was constructed over it, initially called Park Road but this name was soon changed to Westgate Street.

During the 1850s Cardiff began to surge ahead in terms of population and trade, notably coal exports. From the 1850s, the vast steam coal reserves of the Rhondda were opened up, and so great was the demand for the 'black gold' that a new dock, the Bute East Dock, was opened in 1859. The tonnage of coal exported rose from 661,382 in 1850 to 1,802,450 by 1860. The population grew in tandem with this from 18,351 in 1851 to 57,363 by 1871. From this point onwards Cardiff became Wales's largest town. People moved in from rural Wales, Ireland, border

Kingdom Brunel. Work began in 1849 and by 1853 the river was taking its present course through the centre of Cardiff. The Great Park, or as it was increasingly being known as, the Arms Park after the nearby coaching inn, had doubled in size with a huge southward extension onto the

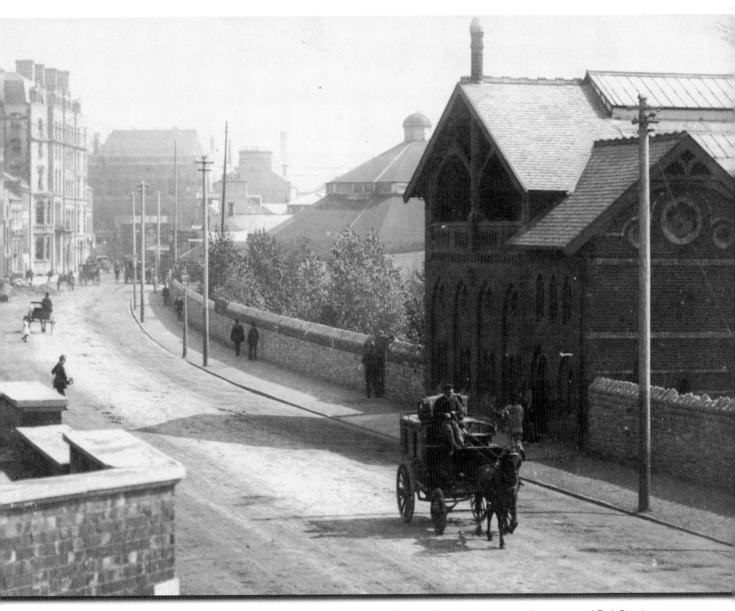

This view down Westgate Street is from the position of the old town quay. After the river diversion, the new road was renamed Park Street but this was soon changed to Westgate Street to commemorate the medieval gateway that stood near the top of the street. The chalet-roofed building was originally a racquets club, opened in 1878, and is now owned by the WRU, while the pyramid style structure behind it housed a circus.

Temperance Town viewed from Cardiff Castle in about 1890. In the foreground the ancient Womanby Street winds through what had been the town's quayside district prior to the river diversion. The Arms Park, with the stubborn swamp clearly visible, lies on the other side of Westgate Street.

counties of England and further afield. In many of these places centuries-old traditional ball games had been played. Many of these were of a similar nature, often involving neighbouring communities competing en masse with a wooden ball or bladder across large swathes of countryside. This loosely-controlled mayhem was known as *cnappan* in Wales, *cad* in Ireland and *soule* in France and could involve hundreds even thousands of competitors in a game. In some cases participants were on horseback and some even carried arms. Injuries, even deaths could occur and a game could last a day or more. It was hardly the kind of activity suited to the crowded streets of the new industrial centres like Cardiff. The urban population's sporting energy had to be harnessed and channelled. Therefore, rules were needed.

The model for this existed in the way English public schools used a style of 'football' as physical recreation for their pupils. Different schools had different sets of rules. The principal variations of these rules involved the level of physical violence permitted in stopping an opponent, and whether or not a player could be able to use his hands as well as his feet to control the ball. The rules at Eton College and Harrow School favoured no hands but those at Rugby School did. Students from these schools heading to university at Oxford and especially Cambridge, took their games with them and influenced fellow students, including those from Wales, who in turn brought them back home after their studies. Cambridge was particularly important for Welsh rugby's development as its Nonconformist traditions attracted a large number of Welsh students. In many cases these Welsh students returned to teach at Welsh public schools such as Christ College in Brecon, Llandovery, Monmouth and Lampeter. It was in this way that the game of rugby football came to Wales. The Welsh schools largely adopted the handling game

In 1872 John Crichton-Stuart third Marquess of Bute and Britain's most eligible bachelor, married Gwendoline Fitzalan-Howard, grand daughter of the Duke of Norfolk. Cardiff, heart of the Butes's Welsh domains, celebrated with this curiously rural sports day in an increasingly urban setting. Clearly the name Cardiff Arms Park had supplanted "The Great Park" by the 1870s. Over the next two decades rugby established its unique bond with the park and its iconic name.

Marriage of the Marquis of Bute.

RUSTIC SPORTS

AT THE CARDIFF ARMS PARK,

16th APRIL, 1872, TO COMMENCE AT ONE O'CLOCK.

PROGRAMME.

1. **Flat Race, 100 Yards.**
   First Prize, 2 Guineas. Second Prize, Entrance Fees.

2. **Long Jump.**
   First Prize, 1 Guinea. Second Prize, Entrance Fees.

3. **Putting the Weight.**
   First Prize, 1 Guinea. Second Prize, Entrance Fees.

4. **Flat Race, 200 Yards.**
   First Prize, 2 Guineas. Second Prize, Entrance Fees.

5. **High Jump.**
   First Prize, 1 Guinea. Second Prize, Entrance Fees.

6. **Throwing the Hammer.**
   First Prize, 1 Guinea. Second Prize, Entrance Fees.

7. **Flat Race, Quarter of a Mile.**
   First Prize, 2 Guineas. Second Prize, Entrance Fees.

8. **Tossing the Caber.**
   First Prize, Half-a-Guinea. Second Prize, Entrance Fees.

9. **Hurdle Race, over 12 Flights.**
   First Prize, 2 Guineas. Second Prize, 1 Guinea. Third Prize, Entrance Fees.

10. **High Pole Jump.**
    First Prize, 1 Guinea. Second Prize, Entrance Fees.

11. **Sack Race.**
    First Prize, Half-a-Guinea. Second Prize, Entrance Fees.

12. **Military Hurdle Race, over 12 Flights.**
    First Prize, 2 Guineas. Second Prize, One Guinea.

13. **Three-legged Race, 100 yds.**
    Prize, 2 Guineas to Winners.

14. **Donkey Race.**
    First Prize, 2 Guineas. Second Prize, 1 Guinea. Third Prize, Entrance Fees.

CONDITIONS.

1. All Competitions (with the exception of Military Hurdle Race), open only to Amateurs, who must be residents of the Parliamentary Borough.
2. All Races to be Handicapped.
3. Entries for all Competitions (Sixpence) to be paid to the Committee, at the Town Hall, between the hours of Seven and Nine, p.m. on Monday, 15th instant. Post Entries on the Ground, One Shilling.
4. All Prizes in Money or Plate at the option of the Winner.
5. Four Competitors for each Prize, or no Public Money will be given.
6. Military Hurdle Race open only to Regulars and Militia Men.
7. Donkey Race Jockeys, to ride in Colours to be named at time of entry. Best Donkey to win.

The Sports will be preceded by an **ENTERTAINMENT** by Messrs. **MARTINI & ESTUARDO** on the Ærial Double Bar, the Double Flying Trapeze, with Double and Treble Somersaults, and a Drawing Room Entertainment, commencing at One o'clock precisely.

Chairman of Committee........ Mr. P. BIRD.

Judge.... Mr. T. V. YORATH. | Referee ...... Mr. BELL.
Starter .. Mr. R. J. NICHOLL. | Handicappers . Messrs. RICHES & SPIRIDION

W. G. YORATH, } Secretaries.
FRED. WARE,

in the 1870s and, as pupils graduated and found work in the new urban centres, they set up clubs to continue their sport. During the 1870s a rash of rugby clubs were founded in Wales and, with the rapidly developing rail connections, fixtures became possible between clubs once remote from each other. At this point, rugby in Wales made a quantum leap not repeated elsewhere in the British Isles. It crossed the class boundary and, instead of remaining an upper and middle class sport, it was enthusiastically adopted by all. It spread like wildfire from coastal strongholds like Cardiff, Newport, Swansea and Llanelli and up into the mining valleys. New clubs sprang up on an almost weekly basis. The new Cardiff Club began to play on the Arms Park. It had been formed in 1876 after the merger of the Wanderers, Tredegarville and Glamorgan clubs so that they could better compete with local rivals Newport. The club played at Sophia Gardens initially but then increasingly used the Arms Park. Many of its players were also Cardiff Cricket Club men, so the venue was a familiar one to them. The original playing kit consisted of a black jersey with a pirate skull and crossbones emblazoned on the front to reflect the piratical heritage of Cardiff. However God-fearing mothers and wives of some of the players objected to this 'uncanny image', and the kit was soon changed to the famous Cambridge blue and black, chosen because a number of players were former Cambridge scholars. Matches began to attract crowds who paid for the privilege of watching and

competitions such as the South Wales Challenge Cup were launched in 1877. The organising body for fixtures was the South Wales Football Club (1875) which became the South Wales Football Union in 1878. It organised games against sides such as Gloucester and the South of Ireland, but it was not a national union for Wales. The other nations had formed national unions; the RFU in England (1871), The Scottish Union (1873) and the Irish Union (1875). The story of the formation of the Welsh Rugby Union and its dramatic impact on the Arms Park is the subject of the next chapter.

Chapter 2

The 1870s had seen rugby put down its roots in Wales, but it was the 1880s when the sport began to really flourish. Frustrated by the limited ambitions of the South Wales Football Union, some clubs began to consider the formation of a new national union as had already been established in England, Scotland, and Ireland. The chief protagonist and the 'father' of the WRU was Richard Mullock, secretary of the Newport Club. Under Mullock's stewardship, Newport had become the dominant and most progressive of the Welsh clubs. They had four invincible seasons in their first five years, they won the Welsh Challenge Cup twice, and had a stronger fixture list than the SWFU itself. They were the first club to charge gate money and in 1879 Mullock had even organised an evening match between Newport and Cardiff under electric floodlights at Rodney Parade.

Mullock's vision was for an all Wales national union to play against the other national unions and not just a regional one content to play sides such as Yorkshire or the South of Ireland. A fixture against England was Mullock's target and, with typical vigour, he contacted Welshmen living and playing in England. He found willing support for his idea at other Welsh clubs too, notably Swansea, and in March 1880 a rather cloak-and-dagger meeting took place at the Tenby Hotel, Walter Road, Swansea. Little is known about what took place there or even which clubs were represented. The SWFU, still the governing body, was probably aware of it and may have taken a dim view of the conspirators. Whatever the case, Mullock set about assembling a Welsh team to play England. The match was eventually set for 19 February 1881, at Blackheath in London. So that it would be marked as a new beginning, Mullock decided not to use the SWFU kit of black shirts with a white leek emblem. He chose the now famous red jersey and the three feathers emblem as Wales's new national kit. The Prince of Wales feathers were chosen partly to emphasise that this was not the SWFU's side and partly to give the upstart union the lustre of established respectability. The feathers were already the symbol of the London-based Cymmrodorion Society and the Welch Regiment, so Mullock's team were in good company.

The team selection reflected Mullock's intention for an all-Wales side with players drawn from all areas of Wales. The result was slightly one-sided. England won by 7 goals, a dropped goal, and 6 tries to nil. If the match were to be scored under today's rules, Wales would have lost by the equivalent of 82–0. Despite this setback, Mullock's Men, as the team was known, had established Wales as an international team. The days of the SWFU were numbered. On 12 March 1881, at a meeting at the Castle Hotel in Neath, the Welsh Rugby Football Union was established with Richard Mullock as its first honorary secretary. The clubs represented were: Bangor, Brecon, Cardiff, Lampeter, Llandeilo, Llandovery, Llanelli, Merthyr, Newport, Pontypool and Swansea.

Developments were taking place at the Arms Park as well. In 1880–1 gate receipts from Cardiff club games totalled £130, enough to level and re-turf the Arms Park and build its first ever grandstand, "for the convenience of the spectators and ladies in particular". It had 300 seats and cost £50.00 to build.

On 28 January 1882, Wales played Ireland at Lansdowne Road, Dublin. Hopes were not high but the red jerseys finished triumphant by two goals and two tries to nil. After 26 minutes of the match, Tom Baker Jones (Newport) did something no-one else had done in a Wales jersey before – he scored a try. In December 1882, Wales played its first home international. England were the opponents but the game was not played at Cardiff Arms Park but at St Helen's, Swansea. In fact in the early decades Wales used all the grounds of its 'big four' clubs, namely Cardiff Arms Park, Stradey

FOOTBALL.

WELSH RUGBY UNION.

A meeting was held at the Castle Hotel, Neath, on Saturday last, the following clubs being represented :—Swansea, Lampeter, Llandilo, Cardiff, Newport, Llanelly, Merthyr, Llandovery, Brecon, Pontypool, and Bangor, to consider the question of establishing a Welsh Rugby Union. The chair was taken by Mr Richardson, captain of the Swansea Club, and, after considerable discussion, it was proposed by the Chairman, and seconded by Mr F. Meager (Swansea), that a Welsh Rugby Football Club be formed. This resolution was carried unanimously.—It was proposed by Mr Mullock (Newport), and seconded by Mr Margrave (Llanelly), that Mr C. C. Chambers, president of the Swansea Football Club, be elected president of the Welsh Rugby Football Union for season 1881-2.—The next proposition by the Chairman, and seconded by Mr Mullock, was that Mr E. C. Fry (Cardiff) and Mr C. P. Lewis be elected vice-presidents of the Welsh Rugby Union for the season 1881-2. Carried unanimously. The election of a committee (which will in all probability consist of a member of each club in the union) was left until the next meeting, which will be held during this month.—Mr Forester, Merthyr, proposed, and Mr Knill, Swansea, seconded, that Mr R. Mullock be elected hon. sec. of the Welsh R.F. Union. Carried unanimously. The hon. sec. was instructed to prepare for the next meeting a draft copy of the proposed bye-laws to govern the Union. The annual subscription to the Union was fixed at one guinea, with an entrance fee of one guinea. It was decided that in the International Match with Ireland on the 9th April at Dublin the selection of players be left to the same committee that selected the players for the English match. A vote of thanks to the chairman brought the meeting to a close.

Newspaper cutting shows the report of the meeting at the Castle Hotel, Neath, at which the Welsh Rugby Union was formed in 1881.

The 1st Welsh XV or 'Mullock's Men' as they were known went out to face England at Blackheath on 19 February 1881. They changed in the Princess of Wales public house and apparently enjoyed a few 'warm up' drinks prior to kick off. In a close game England edged out Wales by 82–0 in today's scoring values. Nevertheless, Wales now had a national rugby team and revenge over the old enemy would come.

Cardiff's great rivals Newport were the dominant Welsh club of the era, with several invincible seasons and 5 Welsh Cup wins in a decade. This is the 1884-5 side with the trophy. The Black and Ambers were an innovative club under the guidance of Richard Mullock and were the first club to charge gate money in Wales, the first to have an Anglo-Welsh fixture (versus Blackheath) and the first to hold a floodlit game, 'The Electric Light Match' against Cardiff in 1879. Mullock's influence would soon be felt throughout Welsh rugby.

The father of Welsh international rugby. Richard Mullock, a Newport printer and secretary of the Newport club, was the prime mover in the formation of the WRFU. As secretary of the new union, his 'unique' style of book-keeping sometimes infuriated colleagues but this was more than outweighed by his enthusiasm and determination for an all-Wales national side. Secretary from 1881-1892 he sometimes dipped into his own pocket to keep the fledgling union afloat. He died in relative poverty and obscurity in 1920 but left his country a great sporting legacy. Next to Mullock is one of his trademark postcards inviting a player, H.M. Ingledew, to represent Wales in 1891.

Park, Llanelli until 1893; Rodney Parade, Newport until 1897 and St Helen's, Swansea until 1954. However the Arms Park was soon to establish itself as the main venue for Welsh internationals. This was partly due to increased spending on the ground, and partly due to Cardiff's meteoric growth as the 'Welsh Metropolis'.

Cardiff's surge in population during this period was exceptional. In 1871 it became Wales's largest town with 57,363 people and by 1901

The original grandstand at Cardiff Arms Park had just 300 seats and cost £50. This picture shows its grander (just) replacement's opening on Boxing Day 1885. It cost a mighty £362. The teams lined up ready to play are Cardiff and Liverpool. Cardiff won the match by three points to nil.

Frank Hancock of Frank Hancock's brewery. A rugby playing, beer brewing, adopted Welshman, Hancock's talent was such that Cardiff changed their formation to accommodate him, thus inventing the four threequarter system of play that is now standard all over the rugby world but which began as an experiment at the Arms Park.

164,333 people were living there. Coal exports kept on growing and new docks were opened to meet the worldwide demand for Welsh steam or bituminous coal – the world's finest. The Bute East Dock opened in 1859, Penarth Dock in 1865, the Roath Basin in 1874, the Roath Dock in 1887 and Barry Dock in 1889. By the late 1890s, over 18 million tons of coal per year were being shipped out. People from far and wide were settling in the cosmopolitan port city and this new metropolis, brimming with confidence, was less constrained by tradition than older, more established, urban centres. Cardiff's growth was often compared by contemporary writers to American cities, rather than British ones, and this spirit of enterprise was to find sporting expression on the rugby field. A revolutionary style of play known as the four threequarter system was developed at Cardiff Arms Park and would later be adopted worldwide.

Frank Hancock was part of a Somerset brewing family which transferred production across the Bristol Channel to Wales to quench the

Within a century Cardiff had changed from a sleepy coastal village to the port that much of the world depended on for its fuel. Welsh coal powered the world and the industry transformed Wales into the world's first industrial society.

substantial thirst of Cardiff's growing population. To accommodate his prodigious rugby talent Cardiff played him as a fourth threequarter during the 1883–4 season. The standard formation at the time was: 9 forwards, 3 threequarters, 2 half-backs and a fullback. Cardiff reduced their pack to 8 men to play the extra back. On 23 February 1884, in a match against Gloucester at the Arms Park, Cardiff took the field with the new system. The effect was electrifying and other clubs who came up against them soon adopted it. Within a few seasons the four threequarter system created at Cardiff Arms Park had spread across the rugby world and it remains the standard formation for all rugby teams to this day. Crowds loved it as it produced more attacking rugby and the 'Welsh Way', as it became known, translated into added enthusiasm for the sport, an enthusiasm greatly appreciated by club treasurers. Some of this money was used to upgrade the Arms Park. The original 1881 stand was replaced with a larger one costing £362.00, which opened on Boxing Day 1885. Steel perimeter rope was erected in an attempt to keep out 'street urchins', duckboards were placed around the pitch to prevent spectators disappearing into a quagmire after heavy rain, and a second temporary stand went up on the opposite side. A recognisable sports ground was taking shape. One

Thankfully it's not unusual now but when Tom Jones of Newport scored for Wales against Ireland in 1882 he made history as his country's first try scorer. Try number one was not scored on the green, green grass of home but at Lansdowne Road, Dublin. Wales went on to win by 2 goals and 2 tries to nil.

A postcard depicting the Angel Hotel at the top of Westgate Street. This grand Victorian structure replaced the Cardiff Arms Hotel and served as the changing rooms for international games until 1904. The players then crossed the road to get to the Arms Park on the right of the picture.

Wales's first Triple Crown side contained many of the country's first household names including Gould as captain (centre), the James brothers (seated at front) and WJ Bancroft (two places to Gould's left).

strange omission was the provision of changing rooms. Cardiff used the Queen's or Grand Hotels for club matches, while for internationals Wales used the more salubrious and modern Angel Hotel. The Angel had been built on the site of the Cardiff Arms Hotel which in that period of 'progress' had been demolished in 1878. Its name however had become embedded like a fossil in the rugby ground across the road.

Results for Wales improved slightly and a new generation of players and colourful characters emerged. There was W J Bancroft (Swansea), a

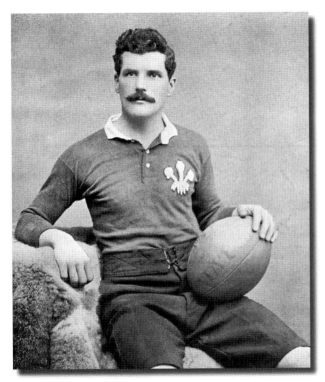

Arthur 'Monkey' Gould of Newport was Welsh rugby's first superstar. The epitome of the Victorian sportsman, his talent made him a hero in Wales and the gifts and donations that flooded in on his retirement in 1897 caused uproar in England, Ireland and Scotland. 'The Gould Affair' gave Wales a sense of pride in standing up to the other unions and resulted in a tacit acceptance by them that Welsh rugby was a little different.

permanent resident at fullback for over a decade who could kick goals from anywhere; the James' brothers Evan and David (Swansea) known as the 'curly headed marmosets' whose trickery at half-back and spontaneous on-field gymnastic displays kept the crowds entertained; Norman

WRFU minutes recording the meeting with the IRB at which the Gould Affair was discussed. Wales's defiance over Gould's testimonial gifts helped define the unique place the game has here as well as the slightly 'different' view of amateur status from the other unions.

The most picturesque of all the buildings to stand on Cardiff Arms Park was the Cricket Pavilion of 1904. It contained a gymnasium and the grounds first changing rooms. Prior to this players had changed in nearby hotels. The Wales and New Zealand teams of 1905 emerged from here to create a mixture of history and legend. The building stood until 1937 and was then dismantled.

Wales's Association Football internationals took place at Wrexham, Swansea and, until 1910, Cardiff Arms Park. This is the Welsh team wearing the rare green and white halved kit of the time.

Biggs (Cardiff) a flying wing from a rugby playing family who went on to become superintendent of Nigeria's police and met perhaps the strangest demise of any Welsh cap when he was ambushed on patrol and killed by a poisoned dart; and C B 'Boomer' Nicholl (Llanelli) a powerhouse forward

and Cambridge scholar who was renowned as 'a connoisseur of exhilarating beverages'. However one name from this period stands out above all others as the first true superstar of Welsh rugby, the incomparable Arthur 'Monkey' Gould (Newport). The Monkey nickname came from his

First Grand Slam Winners —— 1907/8.

childhood prowess at climbing trees, but it was at rugby that Gould's talents really shone. To say that Gould thrust Welsh rugby into the limelight would be something of an understatement. His immense talent, swashbuckling good looks, and inspiring leadership marked him out as a genuine sporting celebrity. By the age of 16 he was already in the Newport XV and was capped by Wales in 1885. Wales had begun to improve with first wins over Scotland by one try to nil at Newport in 1888 and England by the same margin at Dewsbury in 1890. In 1892–3, under Gould's captaincy, Wales won its first Triple Crown and did it playing the 'Welsh Way'. His popularity and fame in Wales and the wider rugby world kept growing. His image appeared on cigarette cards and match boxes, and songs and poems were written about him. In 1896 a testimonial fund started for him by wealthy

E Gwyn Nicholls. Prince Gwyn, captain of Wales and a mastermind of the defeat of the All Blacks in 1905.

Bob Deans, the All Black whose "Try that never was" has been debated for over a century.

Dr Teddy Morgan scored the crucial try to defeat the All Blacks, the only score in the 3–0 result.

Dave Gallagher, New Zealand's popular captain and his fearsome First All Blacks. Gallagher was well liked in Wales and refused to become embroiled in the "The try that never was" controversy. He was killed in action on the Western Front in 1917.

Victorious 1905 Welsh Team.

Two of the most iconic national emblems in world sport. Events at the Arms Park on 16 December 1905 did much to embed rugby at the heart of popular culture in both New Zealand and Wales.

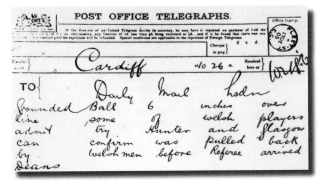

Telegram that sparked the controversy.

The whistle that saved Wales in 1905. When Referee John Dallas of Scotland blew it and awarded a scrum and not Bob Deans's "try" the All Blacks's chance had gone.

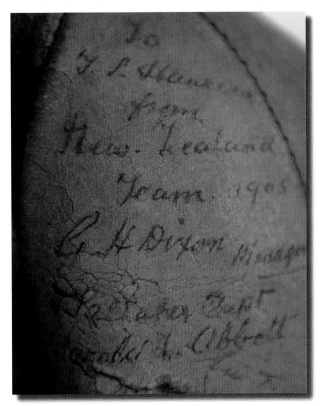

A match ball of the famous 1905 tour.

Decorated and dated corner flags were often produced for a specific game, a tradition which has sadly disappeared in the modern era.

A commemorative postcard reflecting the surge of national pride caused by the 1905 game.

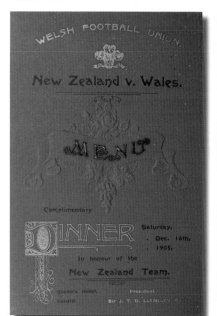

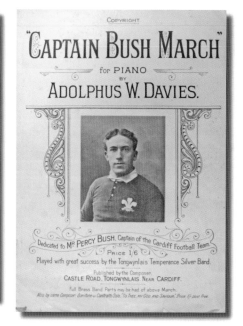

Dinner menu 1905. This is the menu of the dinner held for both teams after the famous match.

The match programme of the famous game which did more than any other in the early decades of rugby to establish the fortress reputation of Cardiff Arms Park.

Players from the victorious side, such as outside half Percy Bush, were lionised by a grateful public.

admirers was boosted by public subscription, and 1,000 shillings even came from the Welsh Rugby Union. The other unions were furious calling Gould a professional and claiming that the Welsh Rugby Union had broken the amateur ethos. The Welsh stood firm and Gould captained Wales to victory over England at Newport in 1897. Subsequently, fixtures were cancelled by England, Ireland, and Scotland, but Wales still stood firm over Gould. To add to the furore, Gould was presented with a house in his native Newport in April 1897. Pressure from English clubs to restart games with the Welsh persuaded the RFU to change its stance. Ireland and Scotland did the same, but the latter not until 1899. Gould kept his house, became a referee, selector and member of the WRFU committee. His contribution to rugby in Wales, on and off the field, was immense and the controversy over his testimonial brought an acceptance that Welsh rugby was somehow a different beast to rugby in the other countries.

One effect of the Gould phenomenon was an increase in gates and revenue. Further improvements were made to the Arms Park. In 1895, drains costing £1,000 were laid underground in an attempt to dry out the boggy morass where the old bed of the river Taff had been and new turf was laid. It was not just rugby which took place on the Arms Park. Association Football was also popular in Wales, and world-class players such as Billy Meredith graced the ground. From 1896 until 1910, Welsh international football

matches took place here, often on Mondays so as not to clash with rugby fixtures. It was not until Cardiff City FC was formed in 1910, with their own ground at Ninian Park, that football left the Arms Park. Cricket, the initial Arms Park sport, also thrived during the summer. Very often rugby and cricket shared players as well as the ground. Glamorgan County Cricket Club had been formed in 1888 and they joined the minor counties league in 1897. They played at various grounds, including Cardiff Arms Park. During this period the Bute family retained ownership of the ground and charged Cardiff rugby and cricket clubs a rental of just 1 shilling per annum, on condition that amateur sports were played.

With the opening of other parks in Cardiff, such as Roath Park (1894), the Butes were happy to see the Arms Park develop more as a sports ground. The developments had to be paid for by Cardiff Rugby Club, but with growing contributions from the WRFU.

The ground certainly needed

1905 medal. These commemorative medals were struck for the victorious Welsh team of the All Blacks game.

A cricket match taking place in front of the elegant pavilion watched by some equally elegant Edwardians. Cricket was a major part of the Arms Park's sporting calendar from the 1840s until 1966 when Glamorgan CCC moved to Sophia Gardens across the Taff. Note the rugby posts on the left.

OPENING OF NEW CARDIFF EXCHANGE FEB. 20th 1912

The First World War had a great effect on the status of women. This photograph shows the Cardiff's Women's team who took on a Newport Women's team in 1917, a match that would have been unthinkable just a few years before.

As the Welsh coal industry approached its zenith, the Coal Exchange in Cardiff's docklands was rebuilt in 1912. The trading floor handled a large percentage of the world's coal trade and was one of the world's most important commercial centres.

The last great success of the 'First Golden Era' was the Grand Slam of 1911. Although no one could have suspected it, it was to be Wales's last Triple Crown for 39 years. The dapper touch judge on the far left is the great AJ 'Monkey' Gould.

expanding. The Wales v Ireland game of 1899 set a world-record crowd of 40,000, packed into a grandstand built to hold 35,000! Spectators climbed walls and fences to get in and some even swam the Taff. In 1900, £1,926 was spent to increase the capacity, with three-quarters of the money coming from the WRFU. The first game in the renovated ground saw Wales defeat England under the captaincy of Gwyn Nicholls (Cardiff). Nicholls and his team were to dominate international rugby in what became known as the first golden era. In the decade that opened the new century, Wales played 35 matches. They won 28

of them, drew 1, lost just 6 and were unbeaten at the Arms Park from 1900 until 1912, a fact that cemented its fortress reputation. Rugby became inextricably linked with Wales both in the minds of the Welsh people themselves and the wider world. Players such as Dickie Owen and Billy Trew (both Swansea), Rhys Gabe (Llanelli and Cardiff) and Jehoida Hodges (Newport) became household names, and leading them was Nicholls who, like Gould before him, was a great tactician and thinker about the game, as well as a superb player. With a mixture of philosophy, science and artistry he refined and developed the 'Welsh Way', resulting

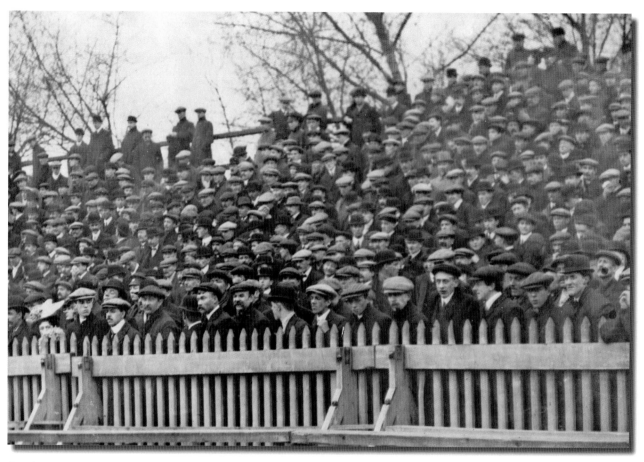

Crowds would pack the terraces long before kick-off to ensure a good view of their heroes. This gave rise to the tradition of hymn singing at Welsh games, as the crowd sang their stirring chapel anthems to keep themselves entertained. This is the crowd for the Wales v Ireland game of 1911. A good time to be in the hat business!

in the strongest rugby team the world had seen. Not for nothing was he known as the 'Prince of Centres'.

One game from this golden era reverberates through the rugby world to this day. On 16 December 1905, Wales played the touring New Zealand team, the first All Blacks. Dave Gallagher's

'Colonials', as they were known, seemed invincible, winning 26 matches out of 26 before their date at the Arms Park. They had dispatched England, Ireland and Scotland but each time had been warned about the Welsh. Wales had just won another Triple Crown and the match was billed as a world championship decider. Public anticipation was whipped up to fever pitch by a hysterical press. The teams emerged from the new cricket pavilion changing rooms at the Arms Park and the match did not disappoint. Described as the greatest game ever, it was fast, fierce, and frenetic and held the 40,000 spectators spellbound. One try decided it and Wales wing Teddy Morgan who scored it, giving the home team a 3–0 win. Intricate preparation by Nicholls and his men had nullified New Zealand's lethal forwards and opened up their defence for the crucial score. It was the All Blacks's only defeat of the tour with 31 wins from 32 matches. What has kept the memory of this epic game alive is the controversy which followed. The following day, a *Daily Mail* reporter, hungry for a story to boost the circulation of this new tabloid paper, suggested to Bob Deans, the New Zealand centre, that when he was tackled close to the Welsh line near the end of the game, he had actually scored and that Scottish referee, J D Dallas, had got it wrong. Deans laughed and said he thought he had scored and the *Daily Mail* ran the story. The debate about the "try that never was" has continued ever since.

Even after Nicholls and his heroes had retired, the production line of rugby talent seemed as healthy as the country's coal industry. This industry produced bone-hard men as forwards to supply rugby backs like Nicholls. These so-called 'Rhondda Forwards' terrified opponents and the other unions often complained that they gave Wales an edge. France joined the championship in

1911 and Wales won the Grand Slam. However some purists complained that the team was now deviating from the 'Welsh Way' and in 1912, the visiting South Africans inflicted the first defeat on Wales at the Arms Park (3–0) in over a decade. In fact, Wales would not win another Triple Crown for 39 years. More ground improvements took place as a new South Stand and new terraces surrounded the pitch at a major cost of £8,000. The prosperity seemed never-ending. Also in 1907, the largest dock in the world, the Alexandra Dock was opened and in 1913 the Port of Cardiff exported 26,139,334 tons of coal. In 1907, the world's first £1 million cheque had been signed in the city's Coal Exchange, which handled about 40 per cent of the world's coal trade. Not surprisingly, coal in Wales was given the nickname of 'Black Gold'.

There was opposition to rugby in Wales (as hard as that is to comprehend), and it came largely from elements in the Nonconformist chapels. Some were worried that rugby clubs were causing men to drink and that the games could become violent affairs. In 1905, the last great surge in Nonconformist evangelism began with a Religious Revival. The leader of the movement was Evan Roberts from Swansea. He was part-preacher, part-mystic and he described rugby as a game for sinners. The movement was very powerful for a short time and caused some players to give up the game, while at a few places, especially in the Swansea area,

The 'Terrible Eight' doing a passable impersonation of a church choir that completely belies their fierce reputation on the field. Keeping an eye on them is the Reverend Alban Davies in his dog collar and next to him keeping an eye on everything is Walter Rees, WRU secretary from 1896 to 1948.

The end of an era. The match against Scotland at Cardiff Arms Park in 1914 was the last Welsh International before the First World War. Although no one knew it, the game marked the end of an age of confidence and certainty in Welsh rugby. The new Post-War Wales that emerged was a very different place both on and off the field.

some clubs ceased to play. At Ystradgynlais the posts were cut down with axes while in Ynys-y-bŵl, only 15 miles from the Arms Park itself, the whole team were baptised and renounced rugby for three years. Even the greatest Welsh statesman, David Lloyd George, complained in 1895 that "morbid footballism" was distracting Welsh attention from more serious matters. By 1907 though even he had seen the value of rugby's popularity and in a "if you can't beat them, join them" gesture, he visited the Arms Park to watch Cardiff play Blackheath. He declared afterwards: "It is a most extraordinary game. I never saw it before and I must say I think it is more exciting than politics." By 1907, the Religious Revival and Evan Roberts himself were exhausted. The rugby tide, it seemed, was too strong for even religion and politics to resist.

And as if to prove this, the Welsh pack of 1913 and 1914 was even led by a clergyman, the Rev. Alban Davies. They were known as the 'Terrible Eight' and were said to be so brutal that only a man with God on his side could control them. When asked how he coped with their colourful language, Davies retorted that when he put his scrum cap on, he could not hear what they were saying. Their defeat of Ireland 11–3 in 1914 was said to be the roughest game ever played.

Not long afterwards a far greater conflict would sweep the world. The world of 'Monkey' Gould and 'Prince' Gwyn would soon be gone forever. The outbreak of World War I in August 1914 halted club and international games at the Arms Park for five years. A few games did take place. In 1915, a recruiting match between a Welsh XV and an English Barbarians XV raised £200 and encouraged 177 men to enlist in the new Welsh Guards Regiment. A charity boxing event, which included great Welsh fighters such as Jimmy Wilde, Freddie Welsh and Jim Driscoll, was a great success as was a sports tournament for wounded soldiers. One other unusual event during the Great War was the first women's rugby match to take place at the Arms Park, when Cardiff Ladies and Newport Ladies met in 1917. Even the Angel Hotel, one time changing room for the international games, was not immune from the effects of the war. In 1917, it was requisitioned by the US Navy as a 'warship' and briefly became the *USS Chattinouca*.

Among the millions of causalities, the war claimed were 13 men who had worn the red jersey of Wales. They were:

W P Geen (Newport)
B R Lewis (Cambridge University and Swansea)
F L Perrett (Neath)
L A Phillips (Newport)
C M Pritchard (Newport)
C G Taylor (Blackheath)
E G R Thomas (Newport)
H W Thomas (Cambridge University and Swansea)
P D Waller (Newport)
D Watts (Maesteg)
D Westacott (Cardiff)
J L Williams (Cardiff)
R D G Williams (Cambridge University and Newport)

Chapter 3

The world that emerged from the carnage and upheaval of World War I was a very different place from the pre-war Edwardian 'golden age'. However, in Wales, this was not immediately obvious. As the war-torn economies of Europe began to rebuild, it created enormous demand for the country's coal and steel. Productivity and exports soared and by 1920, Cardiff was the world's largest tramp steamer port, with 150 shipping companies and a fleet of over 500 registered vessels. It seemed as though normal service had been resumed and the pre-war optimism had returned. This sense of continuity was reflected on the rugby field with the return of some pre-war players such as Tommy Vile (Newport) and Clem Lewis (Cardiff) and big wins over England and Ireland. But it proved to be a false dawn, both on and off the field, as a serious and sudden decline began to affect both the country's economy and its rugby. Just as in the boom years, when the fortunes of Wales's economy and her rugby had been so interwoven, so their respective fortunes were equally linked in the bleak years that were to follow.

There were huge changes in the air, which had major implications for the Arms Park. The old social order in Cardiff, with the Butes at its head in both industrial dominance and civic patronage, was ending. In 1922, ownership of Cardiff Docks passed to the Great Western Railway and this downsizing of Bute holdings also involved the Arms Park. The fourth Marquess offered Cardiff Cricket and Rugby Clubs first refusal to buy almost the whole of Cardiff Arms Park. Only a narrow strip along Westgate Street was excluded from the sale and retained by the Butes. The price was

The badge of authority. The position of Auditor clearly carried some weight, as the bearer of this leather case was allowed into all matches at the Arms Park.

set at £30,000. The money to buy it was raised through a share and debenture issue from the newly-formed Cardiff Arms Park Company Limited. Cardiff Athletic Club was established as a result of a merger of the rugby and cricket interests, and the ground was leased to them. To help with the costs, the WRU contributed £4,000 in return for the right to continue international matches there for another decade. During this period the WRU also continued to stage at least one international match per year at the St Helen's ground in Swansea. Therefore, heavier investment at the Arms Park was not possible.

The economic crisis of the 1920s now began to exert its influence as wage cuts, strikes, pit closures, and a decline in shipping began to bite. The great Welsh coal bubble had burst, punctured by access to cheaper coal from new fields of eastern Europe, and by the vast amounts of 'free' coal flooding the market due to Germany's war reparations under the terms of the Treaty of Versailles and also, of course, by the unyielding rise of the oil-powered internal combustion engine. In 1920 there were about 270,000 miners in Wales (around 10 per cent of the entire population). By 1930, that number had halved and unemployment soared. The years of economic depression hit Wales particularly hard. Unemployment in Cardiff peaked in the 1930s at 36 per cent but in some areas of the coalfield such as the Rhondda, Merthyr Tydfil and western Monmouthshire it reached about 70 per cent. The south Wales

A constant exodus of players from Wales to Rugby League, not to mention a disjointed selection policy, led to a large increase of players capped by Wales during the 1920s as new combinations were tried in search of elusive success.

coalfield became a political battleground. In 1926, Welsh miners were on strike for eight months, despite almost starvation conditions, and the social tensions that this created sometimes spilt over onto the rugby field, as scores between unemployed miners, strike-breakers and policemen were settled. One referee in the Glyncorrwg area of Glamorgan took to keeping a loaded revolver at his side during matches.

The financial implications of the economic decline for Welsh rugby were immediate and severe. The last thing an unemployed miner or docker struggling to feed his family could do was pay to watch rugby. Gate receipts fell and some clubs struggled to continue at all. In Cardiff, the Athletic Club had to do a deal with a greyhound

A man stands on the corner of Quay Street and Westgate Street (the site of the old town quay), perhaps weighing up if he can afford the price of admittance to the next match. The depression hit Welsh rugby harder than the other Unions as the sport was very much a people's game.

Some things don't change. The expectation, excitement, and enjoyment of international day at the Arms Park are clear to see in the faces of these three supporters.

The Butes's decision to part company with Cardiff Arms Park prompted furious fundraising in Welsh rugby. The Cardiff Arms Park Company Ltd was formed to raise share money and the WRU also weighed in with a hefty contribution to secure international rugby on the ground.

D N Rocyn Jones won just one cap but his name is proudly written into his 1925 jersey. Note Welsh shirts made in Scotland!

A ticket to a battle with the old enemy is worth its weight in gold. England generally had the upper hand in the 1920s but this game ended in a 3-3 draw.

Wales's defeat at Murrayfield in 1926 was not a surprise. In fact Wales did not beat Scotland from 1919 until 1927. The record against Ireland and England was only a little better. These were tough years for supporters who recalled the "Golden Era" of the 1900s when defeat was virtually unknown.

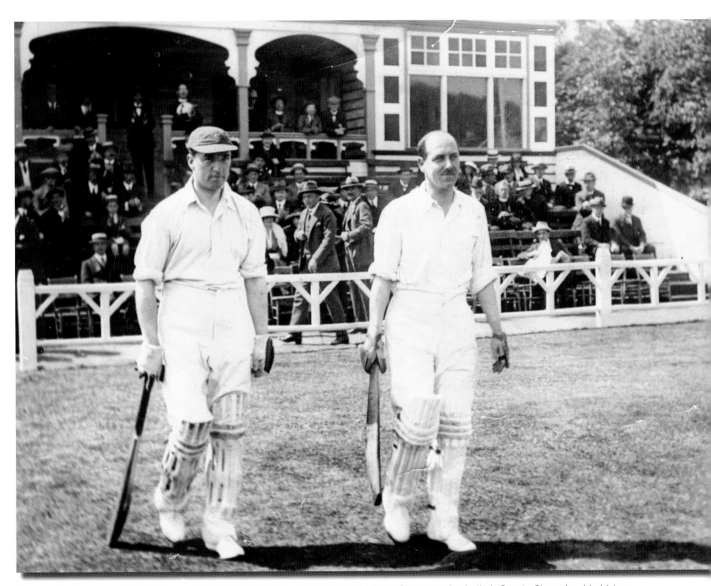

The opening batsman. N V H Riches and T A L Whittington walked to the middle as Glamorgan begin their County Championship history at the Arms Park in 1921. They began with a win. Cricket was the Arms Park's original sport and remained part of the grounds calendar until 1966.

When the All Blacks made their third visit in 1935, few gave Wales a chance. However, Claude Davey's team upset the odds and Wales won a memorable game 13-12.

All Health and Safety Officers – please look away now. Wales v England, 1930. Demand regularly exceeds supply where Wales tickets are concerned and supporters will often go to great lengths, and in this case heights, to see the game.

racing consortium for £2,000 per annum to make ends meet and so dog racing was added to the Arms Park's list of sports. The WRU did make extensions to the grandstand in 1926 with the profits from international matches, but the spectators who sat in them did not have much to cheer about. From 1920–29, Wales played 42 matches – won just 17, drew 3 and lost 22. It was a bitter pill to swallow for a generation brought up on the golden era and the defeat of the All Blacks. In fact the All Blacks returned in 1924, and this time a struggling Wales were no match, going down 19–0, a point for every year since that famous day in 1905. It got worse, with a record defeat to Scotland 35–10, three losses in a row to Ireland for the first time, four in a row to England and in 1928 there was also a first ever defeat to France.

Trial matches often caused more debates than they settled. By the mid 1920s, selection was in the hands of the "Big Five", an inner sanctum of the WRU whose mystical status and power was a cross between that of Old Testament high priests and druids. Their decisions sometimes baffled players and supporters alike.

Hundreds of thousands of people were forced to leave Wales to find work, including no doubt many fine players. There was another serious threat to playing resources and this time it came from the 'other code' of rugby, the professional game, rugby league. It had been established in 1895 when the Northern Union was in a dispute over payment of players. Rugby league had evolved into a different sport, but one with enough surviving similarities to rugby union to make union players a target for

The cap awarded to Wilf Wooller on his Wales debut in 1933.

its talent scouts. Rugby league was a professional game, whereas union remained strictly amateur. A union player who changed codes and took payment was banned for life. Even being caught talking to an agent from rugby league was enough of an offence to be cast out. Nowhere suffered more than Wales from the predations of rugby league.

Talent scouts from its Lancashire and Yorkshire strongholds found rich-pickings amongst the depression-ravaged clubs of Wales. Secret missions by talent scouts, rumours of agents with northern English accents at matches or staying in local hotels created an almost 'Cold War' paranoia. The lure of signing-on fees and good wages was too

53

A WELSH VICTORY

ALL BLACKS LOSE A GREAT GAME

FROM OUR RUGBY FOOTBALL CORRESPONDENT

Welsh Rugby football bridged the years at Cardiff on Saturday when New Zealand were beaten by the odd point in 25—two goals and one try (13 points) to one goal, one dropped goal, and one try (12 points).

The story of the match unfolded itself with all the cruel relish of highly-spiced fiction. A ground hardened by frost and

WELSH DIFFICULTIES

Furthermore, as if to emphasize the poverty of Welsh club football, made worse by the almost daily depredations of the Rugby League in combination with the industrial depression in South Wales, it is generally agreed that the best chances of Wales to-day lie in the pace and cleverness of the " exile " backs rather than the home-produced forwards. It may be that the Welsh pack selected from the seven different clubs of Swansea (2), Cardiff, Newport, Cross Keys, Neath, Llanelly, and London Welsh may settle down into an effective scrummaging machine—they have at least the physique to do so—but it is a matter for serious reflection that no one is confident that they can, while the most optimistic only hope that they may learn the lessons of the match before it is too late.

Rugby is such a passion in Wales that there is rarely any middle ground. People are either on the crest of a wave or in the depths of despair. Nothing illustrates this emotional rollercoaster better than these before and after articles about the 1935 All Blacks game.

much to resist for many a Welsh player struggling to secure his family's future. By 1922, about 50 had 'gone north' but many more would follow as the occasional departure then almost turned into a stampede. In the summer of 1922 for example, Pontypool almost lost all its forwards to league before the season had even started. Many international players were amongst the exodus. Men like Ben Beynon (Swansea), Jerry Shea (Pill Harriers and Newport), Bryn Williams (Llanelli) and Will Hodder (Pontypool) were sorely missed. Such was the rate of defections that no settled side could evolve, which seriously undermined Wales's chance of success. The problem was made worse by the WRU's own chaotic selection process which, until 1924, involved a match committee of 13 picking the team. This was then reduced to five selectors, spread geographically around the country. Inevitably, they often pushed for the inclusion of their local players, sometimes resulting in more deserving players being overlooked.

One such player was Albert Jenkins (Llanelli), one of the outstanding players of his era and a rare beacon of light in a dark decade for Wales. He was first capped for Wales in 1920 but was often dropped as other players were tried in his centre position. Elevated to hero status at Stradey Park, people would pay just to watch him, but Wales's selection policy cost him and he should have won more than the 14 caps he did. To his credit, he resisted several offers to turn professional and played his last match for Wales in 1928. Jenkins

was not alone in lifting the gloom, and men like Rowe Harding (Swansea) and Ivor Jones (Llanelli) did their best to restore pride in the red jersey. One important response to the loss of players and decline in fortunes was the establishment of the Welsh Secondary Schools Rugby Union in 1923. This organisation did immense work promoting and organising the game throughout Wales amongst the 'next generation' and was to provide a production line of many future world class players. However the 1920s was, in the main, a decade Welsh rugby was glad to see the back of.

This was not the case for the cricket played at the Arms Park. Tour matches had taken place before against sides such as Yorkshire, Gloucestershire, South Africa and Australia but Welsh cricket's real ambition was to elevate Glamorgan from the Minor Counties League to full County Championship status. This was achieved in 1921 when Glamorgan became the 17th First-Class County. The Welsh county celebrated by winning its first top-level game against Sussex at the Arms Park. Across the city, professional football was weathering the economic storm much better than amateur rugby. In 1927, Cardiff City FC provided the best Welsh sporting moment of the decade by lifting the FA Cup at Wembley. They beat Arsenal 1–0 and gave the success-starved sporting public of Wales something to celebrate.

As the 1930s dawned, rugby's financial problems continued. The Cardiff Arms Park Company had to raise revenue by selling £12,080

The Arms Park in 1935 viewed from the site of present day gate 3 on Westgate Street. The architecture did not impress the Butes in Cardiff Castle who had apartments built to try and block their view of the ground.

Albert Jenkins was one of Wales's greatest players of this era, yet he won only 14 caps. He was sometimes a victim of erratic selection policy.

One that got away. Jim Sullivan from Cardiff became a superstar in the professional code.

of shares to the WRU and granted the Union the right to improve the ground as it wished and to continue staging international matches there until 2032. This headed off the possibility that the WRU might leave the Arms Park altogether. In the early 1930s, this was seriously considered as the WRU looked at sites for a new stadium at Sloper Road in western Cardiff and at Bridgend, around 20 miles away. The Bridgend option was popular with some at the WRU, as it was roughly in the middle of south Wales and was seen as an east/west compromise. Swansea, still a regular international

Cliff Jones was Wales's outstanding fly-half of the 1930s and one of the conquerors of the 1935 All Blacks. During his career, he suffered numerous injuries including two broken ankles, a broken collar bone, a broken elbow and a broken wrist; but still won 13 caps.

Wales and England have competed against each other at just about every sport, many of them at Cardiff Arms Park. Perhaps one of the lesser known rivalries is in baseball.

venue, also tabled an ambitious bid to become Welsh international rugby's main home. It should be remembered that Cardiff was not yet Wales's capital city (not until 1955), despite having the largest population of Wales's towns and cities, so Swansea's bid was by no means without hope or support. However by 1932, the WRU had settled on Cardiff Arms Park as the focus of its plans, ironically due in no small part to lobbying from clubs in the west of Wales who enjoyed the greater allocation of tickets a Cardiff game afforded, and who no doubt enjoyed their visits to the exotic delights of Cardiff. The North Stand was rebuilt and ground capacity rose to 52,000. The new stand which cost £20,000 was backed by dark, corrugated iron and the view of this from Cardiff Castle offended the aesthetic sensibilities of the Butes. They, therefore, allowed the construction of the apartments on Westgate Street to mask the stadium. Cardiff and Wales had, since the earliest games, shared the same pitch and the wear and tear of this, combined with the boggy ground created a far from ideal surface. One commentator joked that lifebelts should be issued to the players. Despite this, the standard and style of play on view at the Arms Park began to improve again.

In 1933, Wales won at Twickenham for the first time, under the captaincy of Watkin Thomas (Llanelli). Thomas was already a hero for scoring the winning try against Scotland in 1931, despite having broken his collarbone in the game. In

1935, the All Blacks were back again. Hopes were not high for Wales, who had lost to South Africa 8–3 at Swansea in 1931. However the Swansea club side had beaten the All Blacks under the astute leadership of Claude Davey and the centre repeated the trick in the red of Wales as the tourists were defeated 13–12. He had a strong team around him including Wilf Wooller (Rydal School, Sale, Cambridge University and Cardiff), Hayden Tanner (Swansea), Cliff Jones (Cambridge University and Cardiff), and Don Tarr (Swansea) at hooker, who suffered a broken neck with 10 minutes to go. Wales was back and the Arms Park again assumed the role of a fortress. In 1936, the championship was won with a tense 3–0 win over Ireland. The Welsh public were so desperate for success that about 70,000 people overwhelmed the turnstiles and crammed inside, some of them wading and swimming across the river Taff to get in.

The following year, the picturesque old cricket pavilion which had served as changing rooms since the days of Gwyn Nicholls, was removed and new changing rooms built inside the grandstand. The players did not get much chance to use them – the 11–3 win over Scotland in February 1939 was the last international at the Arms Park for nearly 8 years. The 1939–40 season started on 1 September, the same day that Germany invaded Poland. Two days later Britain was at war and the season was abandoned. On 5 September the WRU made its own public declaration: "That this Union,

A wartime cartoon in the South Wales Echo attempts to make light of the bomb damage of 1941. It was far from a laughing matter for the WRU whose new north stand lay in ruins.

Judging from these advertisements it was a great source of pride for contractors to say that they had been part of the rebuilding work at Cardiff Arms Park in the 1930s.

together with its subsidiary organisations and affiliated clubs, suspend their activities during the period of war or until further notice."

As with World War I, charity and service matches did take place. Teams were raised from players in the military or reserved occupations like mining. The strict ban on rugby union and league players playing together was waived which allowed the Arms Park a rare glimpse of some lost Welsh talents such as Jim Sullivan and Gus Risman. There were also appearances by future stars such as Flying Officer Bleddyn Williams (Cardiff). Sadly the Arms Park was not to escape the aerial bombing. On 2 January 1941 at 6.37 p.m., the Cardiff sirens sounded red alert on one of the 585 such occasions of the war. Parachute mines, high explosives and incendiary devices rained down on the city causing great damage. One hundred and sixty-five people were killed that night and over a thousand more injured. Amongst the buildings damaged were Llandaff Cathedral, and Welsh rugby's own 'cathedral' – Cardiff Arms Park. A parachute mine, perhaps intended for the Curran's armament works downstream hit the new North Stand, virtually destroying it. Parts of the South Stand and West Terrace were also damaged. Due to the damage, the profitable service matches had to stop and by the end of the war, the WRU had debts of £40,700 and a wreck of a stadium. One sport did manage to take place on a section of the Arms Park during the later war years, and that was boxing. On 12 August 1944, Swansea's Ronnie

James won the British Lightweight crown from Eric Boon in boxing's first title fight at the ground. With the end of World War II in August 1945, the massive task of re-construction, both on and off the field, could begin.

The following Welsh internationals were killed in action during World War II:

C R Davies (London Welsh)
J R Evans (Newport)
M J Turnbull (Cardiff)

Chapter 4

Sport at the Arms Park burst back into life in September 1945 with the re-commencement of official club rugby. The international championship had to wait until 1947 as the huge readjustment from 'total war' to normality took place. However there were victory matches to cater to the demand of a sport-starved public, which raised valuable revenue for the WRU. The most notable of these was the tour of the New Zealand Army side, captained by Charles Saxton, who visited the Arms Park in 1946. Saxton's mantra was that 'the object of rugby is for fourteen men to give the fifteenth a start of half a yard'. They defeated Wales 11–3, and their attacking style drew huge appreciation from the Welsh public. The Kiwis had brought the 'Welsh Way' back to the Arms Park, and it was a lesson not lost on either the WRU or its clubs.

In the seasons following the war, the Cardiff club was the dominant force in Wales. Thanks to the efforts of men like Hubert Johnson, who kept fixtures going whenever possible through the war, and the fact that they had a number of players in reserved occupations, Cardiff were best-placed to hit the ground running in 1945. They also had a generation of players with great talent, such as Billy Cleaver, Jack Matthews and Bleddyn

Williams. They were joined by Haydn Tanner from Swansea, a fine scrum half who had been capped for Wales in 1935 and went on to represent his country until 1949. His 26 caps would have been many more, but for the war years. Cardiff now set the standard for the other sides to match, and a visit to their Arms Park fortress would be a daunting prospect in these seasons. In the first four seasons after the war the Blue and Blacks won 140 out of 166 games.

The post-war situation in Wales was very different from that which followed the Great War. The country's economic base was far wider and, although coal was still a major industry, the over-dependence on it was gone. The close link between coal's fortunes and Welsh rugby's was disappearing. In fact, although production of coal rose, the number of miners fell, as modernisation occurred. New jobs in light industry and engineering replaced mining jobs and the post-war rebuilding led to near full employment. By 1955, there were just 13,400 registered unemployed in the whole of Wales. There were big changes in society with more women working, a new National Health Service introduced by Aneurin Bevan and the nationalisation of major industries such as coal.

This last change brought the curtain down on the era of the industrial aristocracy, which in Cardiff's case meant the Butes, the family who had created Cardiff Arms Park. On 10 September 1947 the fifth Marquess lowered his family's standard at Cardiff Castle for the last time. The castle and its magnificent grounds, Bute Park, were given to the people of the city and the Bute association with Cardiff, which had lasted 180 years, was over.

This period of hope and relative prosperity bore fruit at the ground in terms of large crowds for club and international matches. The WRU issued a directive to its clubs in 1949, 'to adhere to the true spirit of the open game' and to 'abolish the win at all costs spirit'. The bomb craters were filled in and in March 1949 the War Damage Commission agreed to the re-commissioning of the wrecked North Stand. An eager public, keen to enjoy the resumption of Welsh rugby's unique club rivalries, flocked through the turnstiles. No fixture typified this more than the oldest derby match in Wales between the 'sister ports' of Newport and Cardiff. Big crowds turned out at both Rodney Parade and Cardiff Arms Park to watch the Blue and Blacks take on the Black and Ambers and, on a wintry February day in 1951, 48,500 headed to the Arms Park to watch Newport defeat their rivals 8–3 during a hailstorm. The figure was a world record for a club game at the time and is even more remarkable for the fact that the sides met four times a season. It remains a record for a 'friendly' fixture to this day.

Fresh off a freezing training pitch is Cliff Morgan. Morgan won 29 caps at outside half from 1951-58 and after retiring became a popular commentator and broadcaster. He rose to become Head of Outside Broadcast at the BBC.

Wales was getting back towards the top of the world game, but despite the resurgence at club level in the late 1940s, international success proved elusive. There were high points, such as the 6–0 win over Australia, the tour that saw the Arms Park host the first ever Barbarians fixture against a touring side, but no Triple Crowns or Grand Slams.

Glamorgan's County Championship winners take the field in 1948. The reorganisation of Glamorgan Cricket Club in the 1930s by Maurice Turnbull bore fruit after the war as the Welsh county, led by Wilf Wooller, won their first title. Wooller and Turnbull had both represented Wales at rugby as well. Sadly Turnbull did not live to see the result of his work having been killed in action in 1944.

Next door on the cricket ground, however, there was a huge success for the Arms Park's original sport, cricket. Glamorgan had struggled since joining the County Championship elite in 1921, but training and coaching had been revolutionised at the club in the 1930s by Maurice Turnbull. Turnbull, who had combined cricketing for

Glamorgan with playing rugby for Cardiff, as well as winning two Welsh caps in 1933, sadly never saw the fruit of his labours as he had been killed in action in Normandy in 1944. Nevertheless, his vision led to Glamorgan taking the cricket world by storm in 1948, when they won the County Championship. They were led by Wilf Wooller,

Newport, Wales and Lions wing and Olympic sprinter Ken Jones races over to score what is still the last Welsh winning try against the All Blacks in the 13-8 win in 1953. There was also an important 'first' for this match, as it was the first game at the Arms Park to be televised live.

Haydn Tanner passes from the base of a Welsh scrum against England at the Arms Park. In a long career interrupted by the war Tanner won 26 caps from 1935 until 1949. His first cap was as a schoolboy at Gowerton, from where he joined Swansea and later Cardiff.

An embroidered corner flag from the 1950 Grand Slam season.

another former Wales rugby international and veteran of the 1935 win over the All Blacks, and the rugby connections didn't stop there as Glamorgan inventively adapted the long corridors of the North Stand to become an indoor (albeit very cold) winter training area by carpeting the floor with matting.

It was not long before rugby joined the cricketers in tasting success. The promise of the 1940s was realised in 1950, when Wales won its first Grand Slam for 39 years under the thoughtful captaincy of John Gwilliam (Cambridge University, Newport, Edinburgh Wanderers and Gloucester). The key game was the Triple Crown match against

Wales's 1952 Grand Slam winning team.

a strong Irish team in Belfast which Wales edged 6–3. The victory celebrations did not last long as tragedy struck soon afterwards. An Avro Tudor V aircraft, carrying Welsh supporters home, crashed close to its destination at Llandow Airfield to the west of Cardiff. Only three of the eighty-three passengers survived. One of them, Handel Rogers, went on to become WRU President years later. It was, at the time, the world's worst civil aviation accident, and celebration of the team's achievement gave way to huge sadness across the rugby world. A disaster fund was set up which raised over £40,000, a huge sum at the time. Two weeks later a packed but subdued Arms Park fell silent, as five buglers played the last post before the Grand Slam match with France. Wales went on to win 21–0.

In style, the Welsh side of the period resembled that of the golden era. The pack had a hard edge with players like Rees Stephens

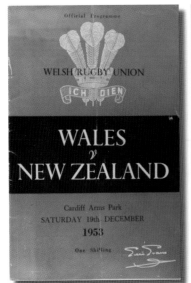

The match programme from the All Blacks defeat to Wales in 1953 and a tour blazer badge from the New Zealanders with the signature of Bleddyn Wiliams. Williams from nearby Taffs Well holds the distinction of leading two sides to victory over the All Blacks having captained Cardiff and Wales in wins in 1953.

and Roy John (Neath) known as the 'terrible twins', D M Davies (Somerset Police) and R T Evans (Newport). They provided ammunition for an attacking back division which included Cliff Davies, Billy Cleaver, Jack Matthews and Rex Willis (Cardiff), Malcolm Thomas and the Olympic sprinter Ken Jones (Newport) and Lewis Jones (Devonport Services and Llanelli). In 1952 another star emerged from the Arms Park in the darting form of Cardiff's outside half Cliff Morgan, and the Grand Slam was won again. All eyes now turned to the visit of the 1953 All Blacks, led by Bob Stuart. Fierce up front and

efficient behind, they had been held to just two draws by Swansea and Ulster, but had won every other match except their two visits to the Arms Park where they were defeated twice, by Cardiff and Wales. Cardiff won 8–3 and Wales clinched a dramatic game 13–8. The victorious captain on both occasions was Bleddyn Williams, while Sid Judd crossed for a try in both games. The decisive moment in the international came with five minutes remaining and the scores tied at 8–8. Clem Thomas (Swansea) found himself bottled up near the touchline, turned and kicked a cross-field ball towards Ken Jones, who gathered it on

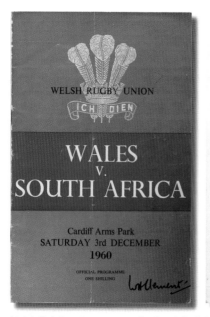

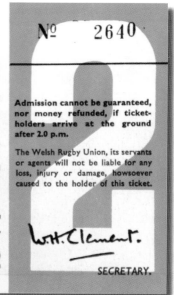

Match ticket and programme for the visit of the Springboks, South Africa's national side, in 1960. The match was played in what many said were the worst conditions of any international after torrential rain had turned the pitch into a quagmire. South Africa won 3-0.

the bounce, cut inside his opposite number and raced under the posts. It was a fitting way to cap what had been a miniature golden era which had re-established the Arms Park at the heart of the nation.

In 1954, the WRU took the decision that Cardiff Arms Park should be the sole venue for Wales's home matches. The extra revenue it could generate meant that the 15–3 win over Scotland that year was the last championship match to be held at Swansea's St Helen's ground. The decision was not welcomed by all, and some critics pointed out, not unreasonably, that the well-drained, fast and sandy pitch at St Helens was better suited

to the open game Wales was espousing than the Arms Park, which could become a quagmire in poor weather. This problem was actually worsening, as many of the underground drains built to carry water away from the pitch had been shattered during the wartime bombing. In wet conditions, players were reduced to lumbering brown hulks, whose own mothers would have trouble identifying them. A Wales v Ireland game in 1957 was halted on the order of the referee, so the players could change into a new kit, as he was no longer able to tell the teams apart. Despite this, and when the weather allowed, Wales did play some exhilarating rugby in the 1950s and of

Even their own mothers would have trouble recognising the players being led off a morass of a pitch by Clem Thomas after this Championship match in Cardiff.

the 18 matches played at the Arms Park in that decade, 14 were wins.

There were improvements off the field as well, with the last of the bomb damage repaired (although Bleddyn Williams maintained the craters filled in at the eastern end always had a nasty stench afterwards). In 1956, a new South Stand was opened and the capacity reached 60,000. The cost of the work (£60,000) was split between the WRU and Cardiff Athletic Club, with the Union paying 75 per cent of it.

Temporary alterations were made in 1958 to enable the ground to host a unique event in Wales's sporting history, an event that was neither rugby or cricket. In 1958, Cardiff hosted the Empire and Commonwealth Games and the Arms Park was converted into an athletics arena. A 440-yard cinder track was laid around the pitch and a temporary footbridge was laid across the Taff to improve access. To the south of the ground a new swimming and diving complex was built, and was known to generations of Cardiffians as the Empire Pool. It survived until the rebuilding work for the Millennium Stadium in the late 1990s. The games were a great success and remain the largest athletics event ever to have been staged in Wales.

The 1960s were a mixed decade on the field, although huge changes were made off it. In 1960, Avril Malan's South Africa, a team Wales had never beaten, came to tour and played three matches at the Arms Park, against Cardiff, Wales and the Barbarians. The Wales game was played

in arguably the worst conditions in the history of international rugby, with heavy rains reducing the pitch to a mud bath. With fifteen minutes remaining and South Africa ahead 3–0, the referee asked both captains if they wanted to continue. They carried on and the Springboks held on to win in the swamp-like gloom. However the occasion is best remembered for what happened the next day. The Welsh rain continued to fall and the Taff made a determined attempt to rediscover its original course by bursting its banks and surging across the Arms Park. The pitch was soon under five feet of water, but it came a day too late to save Wales. Some measure of Arms Park revenge was gained when the Barbarians, including Haydn Mainwaring (Swansea) and Haydn Morgan (Abertillery), inflicted the tourists's only defeat of the tour 6–0.

The Arms Park was not the fortress it had been in the 1950s for Wales. The All Blacks were back in 1963 with perhaps their strongest ever side under the captaincy of Wilson Whineray, and they beat Wales at the Arms Park for the first time 6–0. They lost just one match on the entire tour, when they were beaten by Newport at Rodney Parade. In 1966 Australia beat Wales at the Arms Park for the first time but there were Triple Crowns to celebrate in 1965 and 1969. Great players from the 1950s continued into the new decade such as Ray Prosser (Pontypool) and Bryn Meredith (Newport) and new talent was discovered from a broad base of clubs: Alun Pask (Abertillery), John Collins (Aberavon), David Watkins and Brian Price

(Newport), Dewi Bebb (Swansea), John Dawes (London Welsh), Terry Price (Llanelli) and Clive Rowlands (Pontypool and Swansea) to name but a few. However, consistency was lacking, and after a heavy defeat on tour to South Africa, the WRU focused its attention on youth development and coaching. The Arms Park was again to be the crucible of innovation which was to transform the global game, just as it had been in the 1880s with the invention of the four threequarter system. In 1967, Ray Williams was appointed coaching organiser, the first such appointment in rugby, as the WRU responded to the changing times the game was experiencing. It was a hugely innovative move and a vital one, as the heavy industries which had been so influential in the development of the game in Wales were declining and the links between them and the game were becoming ever more tenuous. In any case, rugby itself was changing at an accelerating rate, and Wales had just put itself ahead of the game. As if to underline the changing background to the game in Wales, a few days before the 1964–5 season began, a coaster, the *Faringay*, pulled away from the Queen Alexandra Dock on 25 August with the last large cargo of coal to be shipped from Cardiff.

Attention also focused on the Arms Park's crumbling stands and notorious pitch. The WRU again looked at a move to Bridgend and in 1962, plans to locate an all-seater stadium at Island Farm were put before the Union and met with widespread approval. In the city of Cardiff, the

Cardiff Arms Park from the west in 1956. With the war time damage to the grandstand repaired huge crowds flocked into club and international matches. The Arms Park continued to be a venue for a number of different sports. Behind the north stand is the cricket ground, while the greyhound track and its lights are clearly visible around the rugby pitch.

plans were greeted with utter horror. The City Council saw the potential loss of income that the international games brought in and did not want Cardiff to be the only national capital not staging international matches. This would have been a serious blow to the prestige of a city which had only been declared a capital city seven years earlier. Supporters and many club officials were not happy with the proposal either. Comparisons were made suggesting it would be equivalent to England playing in Slough or Ireland in Wicklow. A petition was signed by thousands of people, and a phone poll run by the *Western Mail* gave a two-to-one majority against the move.

Cardiff Athletic Club, led by their president Hubert Johnson, was asked to come up with an alternative and it did so in October 1962. They proposed splitting the Arms Park into two rugby grounds, an international ground for Wales and a club ground for Cardiff. Glamorgan Cricket Club would move out altogether to a new site just across the Taff in Sophia Gardens. The Sophia Gardens site was offered by Cardiff City Council who were naturally keen to ensure the WRU stayed in the city. The council's support for the scheme was crucial, as it would avoid potential planning problems. At the same time, the Island Farm scheme was attracting criticism from the Ministry of Transport over traffic issues, and the move was abandoned. The WRU was to have freehold of its ground for the first time and in return would pay for the new Cardiff club ground and Glamorgan's

Promotional poster for the 1958 Empire and Commonwealth Games in Cardiff. The Arms Park was temporarily converted to serve as the main athletics venue for what was at the time the largest sporting event Wales had staged.

Wales's 1965 Triple Crown-winning side.

relocation. In September 1966, over a century of cricket at the Arms Park came to an end as Glamorgan played Somerset in their last match on the famous ground. Their new home across the river would have much better facilities and better drainage and the move clearly did them no harm as in 1969 they won the County Championship for the second time.

Meanwhile, back at the Arms Park, plans were drawn up by architects Osborn V Webb &

Partners for the WRU's greatest investment to date, the National Stadium. For the first time an entire integrated stadium design was planned in one rebuilding scheme rather than individual independent stands. The costs were to be met by the proceeds from international games, bank loans and the first issue of international debenture tickets. The first debenture subscription was £50 and entitled the holder to buy an international ticket for 50 years. They sold well and with the funds becoming available, demolition began on the old North Stand in 1968 initiating a 16-year construction programme.

Reconstruction was also beginning on the field, as a number of new players were introduced to the Welsh side. This young side fared badly in the 1967 championship and in their final match they faced a strong England side at the Arms Park, needing a win to avoid a first ever 'whitewash'. The Welsh side included inexperienced players such as Gareth Edwards and Gerald Davies (Cardiff), John Taylor (London Welsh) and 18-year-old Keith Jarrett of Newport, who had only left school a few months previously, making his debut. To make the Welsh crowd even more nervous Jarrett, a centre, was selected out of position at fullback. In true fairy tale style the young side was

In the early hours of 4 December, 1960, after heavy rains, the River Taff made a determined effort to return to its original course and burst its banks. The Arms Park was soon under five feet of water but sadly it came a day too late to save Wales from a 3-0 defeat by South Africa.

unstoppable, with Gerald Davies scoring twice and Keith Jarrett producing the man of the match display, scoring 19 points including a famous 60-yard try as Wales won 34–21.

The new 'stage' being constructed at the Arms Park and the new 'cast' of players being assembled to perform on it were about to turn the National Stadium, Cardiff Arms Park into one of the most compelling arenas in world sport.

Demolition work on the old North Stand began in 1968 to begin a 17-year reconstruction process. Cricket had moved to Sophia Gardens and two rugby grounds were created instead of one. One was a club ground for Cardiff RFC and the other the National Stadium for Wales.

Chapter 5

The Triple Crown of 1969 and the coaching revolution in Welsh rugby ushered in a new feeling of optimism. This was helped considerably by the coming together of a number of extremely gifted players who would justify this optimism many times over during the next decade. The style of rugby envisaged by the WRU would need an Arms Park fit to stage it and, in particular, a pitch capable of allowing it. As the concrete cradle of the new stadium began to grow in the Cardiff skyline, the decade opened with the visit of the South Africans. As if to remind everyone why the new ground was needed, the rains and the mud reunited for one final time to produce another soup-like surface. South African visitors who attended fixtures at the Arms Park could have been forgiven for thinking Wales must be inhabited by a race of web-footed amphibians, as the fixture seemed cursed by heavy rain. In fact, the conditions probably harmed Wales's chances more than the visitors, as any attempt at open rugby sank in the mud. With Wales trailing 6–3, and just minutes to go, a brown shape resembling Gareth Edwards emerged from the morass to splash down in the corner and the match ended 6–6. Despite being

Wales's best result against South Africa the feeling was one of frustration that a potential win had been missed.

It had not been a happy tour for the South Africans. Protests over the apartheid system were seen wherever they played, including quite violent scenes in Swansea. Fears of a similar protest at the Arms Park led to a cordon of barbed wire surrounding the pitch for the test match. The team had already lost two games in Wales, going down 14–8 against a 'Gwent' XV and losing for the second time to Newport 11–6. All this added to the frustration at the drawn match and focused attention on the state of the pitch.

The new National Stadium soon gained a reputation for a superb playing surface, arguably the best in the world. With Cardiff RFC now playing on a new ground next door, the grass had time to recover and thrive as the WRU planned for only around ten games per season to take place on the 'hallowed turf'. They also employed a dedicated team of ground staff, led by Bill Hardiman, whose pitches became the envy of the world. With millions now watching the verdant field on colour television, the image of the muddy

The National Stadium under contruction. Work on the new ground lasted for 17 years as the 'concrete cradle' design slowly encircled the home of Welsh rugby. It was finally completed in 1984 but just 13 years later it was demolished to make way for the Millennium Stadium, finished in just 30 months.

quagmire of the old ground could now become a distant memory. This dramatic change is best summed up by an interview with Graham Mourie, the popular New Zealand captain of the 1978 tour. Mourie was asked if there were similar pitches in

New Zealand. He replied that there were – but that they were used for tennis and bowls.

Engulfing the carefully manicured field was the growing shape of the new stadium. The design consisted of a large upper-tier of seating

Wales's 1969 Triple Crown triumph ushered in a second Golden Era for the national game.

above a lower-tier containing terraced and seating areas, which was to enclose three sides of the pitch on the north, west and south. The eastern end would be an uncovered two-tier terrace to boost the capacity and satisfy the preference for standing that many rugby fans had. As the 1970s progressed, the slow growth towards the 65,000 capacity continued. For parts of the decade the ground resembled a building site, but what was taking place on the field distracted attention from

Barry John alias "the king" is regarded by many as Wales's greatest Number 10. There were many other contenders for this title however, all products of the mythical "outside half factory".

players during the course of the championship and the team became so familiar that the players became national figures. At outside half the mercurial Barry John (Llanelli and Cardiff) was almost venerated by the Welsh support and earned the epithet of 'the king'. J P R Williams (London Welsh and Bridgend) became an ever-present at fullback, going on to win 55 caps. In the process he revolutionised fullback play as an attacking as well as defensive role. Before him, only two Welsh fullbacks had ever scored tries, Viv Jenkins in 1934 and Keith Jarrett in 1967. Williams scored six tries from fullback and his tackling at the other end saved many more. Mervyn Davies (Swansea) was a hugely respected number 8, whose attacking flair and hard tackling gained world renown. Nicknamed 'Merv the Swerve', his line-out and loose play were a huge asset to Wales until illness sadly caused an early end to his career in 1976.The quiet man of the side, but one hugely respected by his team mates, was Dai Morris (Neath), a flanker whose tireless support play earned him the admiration of the Arms Park crowds who christened him 'the shadow'. Morris was something of a rarity in the Welsh team at this time, in that he worked in a colliery. The team now contained more sons of miners than miners themselves. Such had been the fundamental change in the Welsh economy during the middle decades of the century, that a miner in the side was now almost regarded with a sense of nostalgia. By 1979, there were barely 30,000

that, as it matched anything seen at the Arms Park over the previous century.

In 1971, the Grand Slam was won under the captaincy of John Dawes. Wales used just 16

The match that clinched the third Grand Slam of the 1970s.

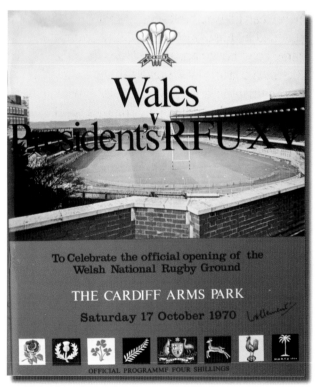

The proportion of female supporters grew during the 1970s and 1980s. This fan's allegiance is not in any doubt!

A match against an invitation XV to celebrate the first phase of the new ground. Matches such as this brought in valuable revenue to help with the long rebuilding process.

miners in Wales, a drop of about 240,000 since the early 1920s. Two sons of miners in the side were Gareth Edwards and Gerald Davies. Davies provided a lethal cutting edge on the wing, where his electrifying sidestep frequently left would-be tacklers holding armfuls of air. Edwards, at scrum half, was the pivotal link in the side. He went on to win 53 consecutive caps and has been consistently voted the greatest rugby player of all time. He became a totemic figure, not just in Welsh rugby but in Wales in general, during this period.

In 1971, the successful British Isles tour to New Zealand was built around this side and coached by another Welsh great, Carwyn James. James had been capped by Wales in 1958 but it was as a coach that he really shone, where his commitment to attacking rugby and meticulous preparation made him one of rugby's great strategists. Sadly, he was never chosen by the WRU to coach Wales. He did coach one Welsh side to victory over the All Blacks however, when his Llanelli side defeated the 1972 tourists 9–3 to add their name to those of Swansea, Cardiff and Newport in overcoming the toughest of opponents. That defeat however seemed to make the All Blacks even more determined, and in a bad-tempered game at the Arms Park, Wales went down 19–16. The 1972–3 New Zealand tour ended in the traditional battle with the Barbarians and the match proving to be one of the most famous in the Arms Park's history, with a candidate also for the greatest try. The try was begun near his own line by Phil Bennett (Llanelli), the equally elusive successor to Barry John, and finished in dramatic style by Gareth Edwards. The Barbarians won it 23–11, so the Arms Park could at least claim a measure of revenge for the test defeat.

The advances in coaching, continuity of selection, some exceptionally talented players and a surface perfect for attacking rugby combined to keep Wales at the forefront of the game. Crowds arrived at the national stadium expecting victory and were rarely disappointed. After another successful (and heavily Welsh influenced) British Isles tour in 1974, this time to South Africa, the serious business of winning the Five Nations Championship resumed. More Grand Slams followed in 1976 and 1978 and the Triple Crown was held for four seasons from 1976–9. The conveyer belt of talented players like: J J Williams (Bridgend and Llanelli), Ray Gravell and

Mervyn Davies an icon of Welsh rugby in the 1970's, "Merv the Swerve" complete with his famous headband led Wales to the 1976 Grand Slam. Many players of this era were simply known by their Christian names, there was no need for a surname as everyone knew who you were talking about.

Phil Bennett the mercurial successor to Barry John and another from the production line of the "outside half factory". Bennett's jinking runs terrorised opponents until his retirement after the 1978 Grand Slam.

Derek Quinnell (Llanelli), Allan Martin (Aberavon), Geoff Wheel (Swansea), Steve Fenwick (Bridgend), Jeff Squire (Newport and Pontypool) and the terrifying triumvirate of the Pontypool Front Row, namely Graham Price, Bobby Windsor and Charlie Faulkner, became household names, not just in Wales but wherever the game was played.

BBC broadcasts of the matches in colour, combined with the magnificent commentaries of

Bill McLaren, gave the players and the stadium a level of fame and recognition not seen in the game previously. Players were known simply by their first names, nicknames or just initials by millions of people, many of whom had never picked up a rugby ball or visited the Arms Park. This, the second golden era, as it became known, was unlike any other in the ground's history. However the link with the original golden era of the early 1900s can clearly be seen in

Gerald Davies in determined mood was a daunting sight for visiting defences at the Arms Park. He had electrifying pace and it was rumoured that he could side step an opponent in a phone box.

Gareth Edwards, another player known only by his Christian name, shown here after scoring one of the greatest tries in the Arms Park's history against Scotland in 1972. Consistently voted the greatest international player of all time, he was an ever-present in the second Golden Era and won 53 consecutive caps.

its importance to Welsh identity. The 1900s, a period of economic growth and confidence, saw Wales establish itself as rugby power, and the game became inextricably linked with the country's sense of identity. In the 1970s, by contrast, a period of economic uncertainty and much internal argument about Wales's future direction, the achievements of the national side were a reliable source of pride and confidence. The strong sense that these men in red were

doing just a little bit more than playing a rugby match when they ran out onto the famous pitch, is best illustrated by the famous team-talk given by Wales's captain Phil Bennett prior to the win over England in 1977, which contained the lines: "Look at what these bastards have done to Wales. They've taken our coal, our water, our steel. They buy our homes and live in them for a fortnight every year. What have they given us? Absolutely nothing. We've been exploited, raped,

Ray Gravell was a strong tackling, strong running centre who gave Wales a hard edge in midfield. His powerful attacking charges set up countless chances for the players around him during his 23 caps from 1975 to 1982. He went on the 1980 Lions tour to South Africa and played in all four tests.

Dai Morris was not the biggest back row forward in the world but pound for pound he was probably the strongest. He was also extremely fit, often finishing a shift as a coal miner to begin training with Wales without a break. Morris had such an uncanny ability to be in the support of the ball carrier that at times there seemed to be two of him on the field and it earned him the nickname "the shadow" from his team mates. He won 34 caps between 1967 and 1974.

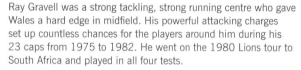

controlled and punished by the English… and that's who you are playing this afternoon."

The 1978 Grand Slam win over France marked the retirement of Gareth Edwards, Gerald Davies and Phil Bennett. However, the production line seemed to be functioning well, especially at the Arms Park, as Cardiff half backs Terry Holmes and Gareth Davies stepped in to fill the illustrious boots. The first big test came in

late 1978 with the visit of the All Blacks led by Graham Mourie. Just as in the first golden era, the New Zealand match would provide the Arms Park with another moment of high controversy. In the closing minutes of the match, with Wales narrowly ahead 12–10, New Zealand forwards Andy Haden and Frank Oliver hurtled theatrically out of a line-out, as if they had been pushed. Referee Roger Quittenton blew his whistle and

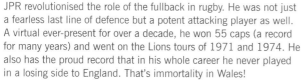

JPR revolutionised the role of the fullback in rugby. He was not just a fearless last line of defence but a potent attacking player as well. A virtual ever-present for over a decade, he won 55 caps (a record for many years) and went on the Lions tours of 1971 and 1974. He also has the proud record that in his whole career he never played in a losing side to England. That's immortality in Wales!

Graham Price, Bobby Windsor and Charlie Faulkner were fierce enough on their own but as a unit they were a triumvirate of terror for visiting opponents. Without the platform they provided the dazzling back play Wales produced in this era would not have happened. As a unit, they represented Wales 19 times and all three also toured with the Lions. The "dark arts" of front row play were never so popular.

signalled a penalty to New Zealand as the Welsh players looked on in bewilderment. Television replays showed viewers at home what many in the stadium suspected, that Haden and Oliver had tricked the referee into giving the penalty. Brian McKechnie duly stepped up and kicked the goal and the All Blacks won 13–12, to the dismay of the crowd. Controversy raged with accusations and denials of cheating, just as they had after the

same fixture 73 years earlier. To make matters worse, Haden later admitted in his autobiography that the falls were a premeditated move in the event of a close game. It remains one of the most debated moments in the history of Cardiff Arms Park, and to many the defeat marked the beginning of the end of a great period in Welsh rugby. It wasn't quite the end of the successes though, as in 1979 Wales won the Triple Crown

Fans packed the terraces of the 1970s to witness the second golden era of Welsh rugby. Home knitted scarves and bobble hats became Wales's unofficial national dress.

for a fourth successive year to complete a remarkable era. For the record, between 1969 and 1979 Wales had won the Championship outright six times, collecting six Triple Crowns and three Grand Slams.

The Arms Park continued in its role as a place central to the development of the global game. The WRU built a proud reputation of welcoming junior unions to play Wales during this era. Non-capped matches had previously been held against Fiji in 1964 and 1969 with an under-25s game at the ground in 1970. Japan visited in 1973; Tonga in 1974 and Romania in 1979. These were important steps in strengthening the global game and prompted the Romanian team manager to state that, "Wales show their love for the game by their willingness to play anyone". It was also, in no small measure, due to strong lobbying by Wales, that France was belatedly admitted to the IRB in 1978.

Senior club rugby was now taking place next door to the Arms Park at Cardiff RFC's new ground, built on the site of the old cricket field. However, once a season, the first-class club game moved into the national stadium for the final of the WRU's Challenge Cup. The competition had been revived in the 1971–2 season following a gap of about 60 years. Although only a modest 12,000 people watched the first final, in which Neath beat Llanelli 15–9, by the end of the decade, large crowds of supporters and neutrals headed to watch what had rapidly become a major date in the Arms Park calendar. Llanelli established themselves as the cup's specialists, winning the four finals from 1973–6, but by the end of the 1970s Newport, Swansea and Bridgend had all tasted victory on Cup Final day.

The 1980–1 season saw the WRU celebrating its centenary. As well as deserved pride in the achievements of the previous hundred years, there was also anxiety over the substantial amount of money still needed to complete the final phase of the National Stadium project. Up to £4 million needed to be raised to finish the job, and so celebration matches against an Overseas XV and a President's XV were staged both to entertain and raise revenue. It was at this point that New Zealand stepped in to help, with the offer of a test match at the ground, which the WRU gratefully accepted. The game contributed to the rebuilding work of both the stadium and the relationship between the two rugby-dominated nations (which had taken a downward turn after the 1978 match). The All Blacks ran out comfortable winners this time, and the new decade was to prove one of mixed fortunes for Wales.

The weight of expectation on Welsh sides following the successes of the 1970s would be a heavy burden. Wales's innovations in coaching were soon copied by other nations, who uncovered their own talented players, therefore closing the gap on Wales. In 1982, a strong Scotland side visited the National Stadium and won 34–18. It wasn't only the size of the defeat

Ieuan Evans was Wales's most dangerous finisher of the late 1980s and early 1990s. He broke the Welsh try scoring record at the time as well as the captaincy record held previously by AJ "Monkey" Gould for over a century.

Jonathan Davies was another in the mould of Barry John, Dai Watkins and Phil Bennett. His move to Rugby League in 1989 was a hammer blow to Wales. He succeeded in both codes and is now a regular commentator on both.

that shocked the Welsh support, it was the fact that they had been defeated at all. The loss marked the end of an unbeaten home run of 27 matches in the Championship which stretched back to 1968. The Arms Park fortress had been breached. In 1984, Australia avenged their 18–13 defeat in 1981 by running away with a 28–9 victory, which simply underlined the loss of the ground's impregnable reputation. There was some positive news in 1984 however as the National Stadium was finally completed after almost twenty years

of debate, planning and construction. It had cost about £9 million, four times the original estimate, but could now welcome 65,000 supporters to watch the next chapter in the ground's story. Wales's playing record during the 1980s saw the team win 50 per cent of its matches compared to the 70 per cent of the 1970s, but the clamour for tickets remained unchanged and an international ticket for the Arms Park retained its status as a sought-after commodity, often changing hands for far more than its face value.

Neil Jenkins, the "ginger monster", was worth twice his weight in gold to Wales. One of the greatest goal kickers in rugby history, Jenkins broke the world points record in internationals and was the first player to pass 1000 test points. He is currently Wales's kicking coach.

There were memorable games and events to savour as well. In the 22–15 win over Scotland in 1986, the Wales fullback Paul Thorburn (Neath) struck the longest goal ever recorded at the ground from well inside his own half. The kick was measured at a huge 70 yards and 8 inches (64 metres), a record which still stands. Towards the end of the decade there was a revival in fortunes. In 1987, the inaugural Rugby World Cup was held in Australia and New Zealand. A young Welsh side under an experienced

captain, Richard Moriarty (Swansea), did well and progressed to the semi-finals before being defeated by eventual winners New Zealand. The team rallied and defeated the much-fancied Australian side 22–21 to claim the third place play-off. New names began to excite a Welsh public which was by now getting impatient for success. Among those who impressed were: Ieuan Evans (Llanelli), Robert Jones, Paul Moriarty, Richard Webster (Swansea), Dai Young (Swansea and Cardiff), John Devereux (Bridgend and South Glamorgan Institute) and above all Jonathan Davies (Neath, Llanelli and Cardiff) in the outside half jersey, the position which more than any other attracts debate in Wales. The new-look side returned to Wales and won the Triple Crown in 1988 playing an open brand of rugby. Sadly for Wales, it was not just the Arms Park crowd who appreciated their ability. Rugby league scouts were back with a vengeance and the effect of their raids was as damaging as it had been in the 1920s. The problem was compounded by the growing incompatibility of Rugby Union's amateur ethos and the demands on the modern players. The professional code offered a lucrative alternative and the Welsh sides of the late 1980s and early 1990s were repeatedly decimated as players 'went north'. Just as in the 1920s, no settled side could evolve and results suffered. In 1989, Romania beat Wales at the Arms Park 15–9, and the following year, the 1990 Five Nations saw Wales 'whitewashed' for the first time. In

Ian Rush scores the winning goal against Germany in 1991. Association Football once again become a regular sport at The Arms Park after an absence of eight decades.

1991, England won at the Arms Park for the first time since 1963 and worse was to come. In the 1991 World Cup, Wales were stunned 16–13 by Western Samoa and exited at the pool stage. By the time Canada turned up and defeated Wales 26–24 in 1993, the reaction of the crowd was more one of resignation than shock.

Wales could still produce world-class players such as Scott Gibbs (Neath and Swansea), Allan Bateman (Neath) and Scott Quinnell (Llanelli) but just couldn't keep them from the clutches of rugby league and all three of these also 'went north'. In 1994, despite the loss of players, Wales won the Five Nations and the sense of frustration at what might have been achieved, or at least avoided, in this period was felt very keenly by the Welsh public. Two players who remained in rugby union during this period and who did a huge amount to restore pride in the national game were Llanelli's flying wing Ieuan Evans and Neil Jenkins (Pontypridd and Cardiff) at outside half. Both players went on to break numerous records with Evans passing Arthur Gould's total of games as captain, doing the job 28 times, as well as setting a then try-scoring record of 33 for his country. Jenkins became the first player in the history of international rugby to pass a thousand points for his country, and both players were involved in successful British Isles tours.

The 1980s and 1990s saw the Arms Park open its doors to other sports and events. There had been some criticism that it was an underused resource and to truly justify the title of National Stadium, it should do more than stage about ten rugby games each year. In addition, just as in previous times, the WRU was aware that extra revenue could be brought into the game by using its prime asset. Association Football returned to the Arms Park therefore in 1989 after an absence of 79 years when Wales held West Germany 0–0. With the installation of floodlights in 1991 evening matches were now possible.

To celebrate this and to raise revenue to pay for the work, France agreed to a friendly rugby international to officially 'turn on' the lights. This development allowed the Welsh football team to use the stadium for European Championship and World Cup qualifying games and meant increased revenue for the sport as far greater ticket sales were now possible. The move back to the home of Welsh rugby gave the nation's football side a real boost and they achieved some notable results, perhaps most famously, the the 1991 victory over Germany courtesy of an Ian Rush goal. In the qualifying campaign for the 1994 World Cup, Wales came within the width of a crossbar from reaching football's showpiece event for the first time since 1958. Forty thousand fans watched an agonising 2–1 defeat to Romania, which prevented Wales from qualifying. The defeat was all the harder to take, as a late penalty kick by Paul Bodin cannoned back off the crossbar. Despite this, the return of the round ball game to the Arms Park was a successful move.

Boxing also returned to the ground in 1993 for the first time since Ronnie James defeated Eric Boon in 1944. Lennox Lewis met Frank Bruno for the WBC World Heavyweight title and Lewis won in the seventh round. It was the first time in the 20th century that two British fighters had contested a world heavyweight title.

It was during the 1980s that the WRU began to consider the staging of rock concerts at the Arms Park. The superb city centre location and large capacity made the venue attractive to promoters and, despite a failed attempt to put on a Rolling Stones concert in 1982, it wasn't long before the ground established itself on the concert circuit. The first act to perform there was David Bowie in 1987, followed by U2, Michael Jackson, Simple Minds, The Rolling Stones, Status Quo, Dire Straits, Bon Jovi, REM and Tina Turner. There were also two major choir concerts with famous guest performers including Welsh legends Shirley Bassey and Tom Jones. In addition to the rock concerts, religious events were also hosted. In fact from 1975 onwards, the Direct Assembly of the Jehovah's Witnesses visited the stadium and in 1980 the Church in Wales held a service with 30,000 worshippers to mark the 60th anniversary of the disestablishment of the Church of England in Wales.

It was rugby of course that remained the true 'religion' of the Arms Park. However, by the mid 1990s, the game was undergoing huge stresses and changes off the field, largely connected to its continued official amateur status which, to many, was becoming an untenable position. Matters came to a head after the 1995 World Cup in South Africa. Shortly after the tournament the International Rugby Board in the person of Welshman Vernon Pugh brought down the final curtain on the amateur ethos by declaring rugby union to be an 'open' game. Players could now be paid to play the game and there would be no more controversies over testimonials or defections to rugby league. In fact the century-worn path to league was reversed as players headed back to union for its greater rewards and bigger global profile. The announcement was to have major implications for Cardiff Arms Park, as a new age in the story of rugby's most famous setting began.

Chapter 6

Even before the huge changes brought about by the advent of the professional game, a WRU committee had looked into the potential redevelopment of the National Stadium in 1994. Despite the affection in which it was held by Welsh supporters, the stadium increasingly had its shortcomings. It had only been fully complete for a decade but had been designed in the 1960s and its facilities were fairly basic. The East Terrace, for example, was open to the elements and if it rained, as can occasionally happen in Wales, 11,000 spectators got soaked. The ground's capacity was also becoming an issue, as safety regulations meant areas of terracing had been replaced by seating, reducing its capacity from 65,000 to 53,000. This created a shortage of tickets which had been an issue with supporters for some time, but with the advent of the professional game it became one for the WRU as well. Other rugby unions had been busy modernising their grounds. In Scotland, Murrayfield had been rebuilt, the RFU in England had gradually re-modelled and increased the size of Twickenham, while in France the national team was set to move from Parc des Princes to the more modern and larger Stade de France. Wales was in danger of falling behind without a redevelopment of its stadium.

Cardiff in the mid-1990s was in the midst of a period of development unlike anything seen since the zenith of the coal trade. The docks and waterfront of the city were being totally transformed by the Cardiff Bay Development Corporation in the largest maritime urban renewal scheme in Europe. It was against this backdrop of investment and rebuilding that the role of the stadium in the heart of the city began to be considered.

The WRU had three options to choose from, the first of which was to give the existing ground a refit and a face lift. This was rejected as it would not solve the problem of the reduced capacity and resultant low income from ticket sales. In addition, it would not address the problem of future ageing of the stadium, parts of which were already a quarter of a century old. The second solution was the previously considered sale of the site to build a new stadium on cheaper land outside the city. As in the past, this was rejected as it would have caused an outcry amongst supporters unwilling to lose Welsh rugby's traditional home at the Arms

Park. This left the third option of a major rebuild on the existing site. The problem with this was that using the Arms Park site meant no land sale to fund a new stadium, the estimated cost of which was well in excess of £100 million. The projected cost would have made the rebuild an impossibility but, just at the right time, a number of fortuitous circumstances coincided to make the dream of a new ground on the Arms Park site a reality.

The year 1994 saw the launch of the National Lottery. The UK had been slow to establish a lottery – many European countries already had them. It became an immediate success and the large revenue generated was allocated by the Millennium Commission to provided funds for good causes and major landmark buildings. The Commission initially signalled that its first major investment in Wales would be a new and long overdue opera house to be situated in the Cardiff Bay area in order to provide the world famous Welsh National Opera with its first permanent base. However the plan rapidly became dogged by controversy and dispute as the design for the building, known as the Crystal Necklace, by the respected architect Zaha Hadid proved considerably more popular with architecture critics than with the public. There was also criticism that a grant of £50 million would benefit relatively few people if spent on opera. The Commission's strict set of criteria included the need for 'public support' and it was clear that this was something the plan lacked.

It was at this point that Cardiff's Lord Mayor, Russell Goodway, and the Chief Executive of Cardiff City Council, Byron Davies, contacted the Secretary of the WRU, Glanmor Griffiths. They proposed bidding for the available lottery grant to build a new stadium at the Arms Park. The city council were as anxious as they had been on previous occasions not to lose international rugby from Cardiff. They were also keen that the lottery grant earmarked for the unpopular opera house design was not lost to the city altogether. As it turned out their timing was perfect, as the WRU had beaten competition from the southern hemisphere to host the 1999 Rugby World Cup. The prospect that they could be hosting it in a brand new and much improved stadium was too good an opportunity to pass up, and so the WRU, in harness with the city council, made an approach to the Millennium Commission for funding. The initial bid was turned down but a second bid was successful in March 1996 and the planning of the largest and most spectacular stadium in the history of Cardiff Arms Park could begin in earnest.

When the plans were released the ambition and scale of what was proposed surprised everyone in Wales. The new stadium would be reorientated through ninety degrees to run on a north to south axis instead of east to west as all the Arms Park grounds since 1881 had done. It was to include revolutionary features which the builders of the 1881 grandstand could not have envisaged in their wildest dreams. Firstly, there would be a retractable roof to keep out the Welsh winter which, when closed, would create the largest indoor stadium in Europe. Secondly, there would be a removable pitch which would allow the venue to stage a much wider variety of events. The plans by the HOK Lobb Partnership encompassed an area much greater than the existing National Stadium's footprint, and so four large buildings around the stadium would have to be demolished in addition to the stadium itself. The buildings included the city's main telephone exchange, the Territorial Army (TAVRA) headquarters, a large social security office and most controversially, Cardiff's ageing, but popular swimming complex, the Empire Pool from the 1958 Commonwealth Games. Some people questioned the feasibility of the scheme, but in March 1997 the contract to build the stadium was awarded to John Laing Construction with the structural design to be carried out by WS Atkins and Partners. The race was now on to complete the work in the very tight timescale before the 1999 Rugby World Cup.

Obviously it would be impossible for Wales to continue to play at the ground during the construction process, and the last international game held at the old National Stadium was the 1997 defeat to England in the Five Nations Championship. Wales did have the consolation of scoring the last try and points at the ground, when a memorable solo effort by Robert Howley (Bridgend and Cardiff) was converted by Jonathan Davies. The final match at the ground took place

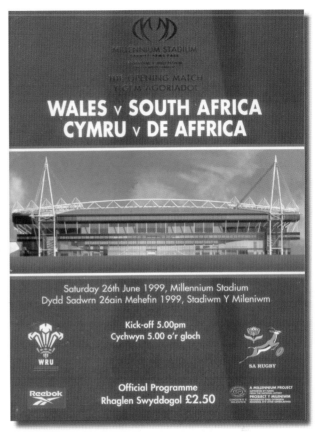

The ticket and programme from the Millennium Stadium's first event the historic win over World Champions South Africa in June 1999.

on 26 April with Cardiff defeating Swansea 33–26 to lift the Swalec Welsh Cup. Many Welsh supporters headed to the game to take one last look at the ground and no doubt to wonder if the new stadium could be completed in less than thirty months before the 1999 World Cup. They also had the chance to buy souvenirs soon afterwards, at a grand auction held in the old stadium. Seats, signs, the stadium clock and even sections of the famous pitch were sold and raised over £130,000 for youth rugby in Wales.

Demolition work began as the bulldozers moved in on the 27 April 1997 and for the next two seasons Welsh international games went into exile in England, as no other ground in the country had the capacity for test rugby. The temporary venue for these 'home' matches was the famous Wembley Stadium in north-west London, the traditional home of the FA Cup and English football.

With Wales's matches now being held in London, Laing's could set about work in Cardiff. They had agreed a fixed price contract with the WRU to deliver the stadium for £99 million which, combined with other costs, brought the total build project to about £160 million. The Millennium Commission weighed in with a crucial £46 million of lottery money and, as a result, the name Millennium Stadium, Cardiff Arms Park was adopted in place of the National Stadium, Cardiff Arms Park. There remained a huge amount of work to get through however, not least the matter for the WRU of raising around £114 million to

pay for everything. This was achieved by selling debentures (guaranteed seats) to supporters for a twenty-five year period and also by arranging a substantial loan of £60 million from Barclays Bank. This was a huge undertaking for a rugby union and the very future of the game in Wales was now effectively tied up with the success or failure of the stadium project.

The central location of the Arms Park had been a huge advantage for supporters and events alike. However, for the contractors at work on the ground the constricted site, hemmed in by Cardiff's club ground, the river Taff and the city centre, made it a difficult logistical challenge. Disruption to the daily life of the city had to be minimised and many nearby properties were fitted with double glazing to mitigate the noise of the rebuilding work. Progress was rapid and within a year most of the old stadium and its familiar 'concrete cradle' outline had vanished. Most, but not all however, as the project hit a major snag. Due to a dispute between Cardiff Athletic Club and the WRU, the increasingly strained relationship between the two organisations broke down to such an extent that the Athletic Club denied the WRU contractors access to the site through their property. As the two sides were unable to reach an agreement, and with time pressure a real issue, the WRU had no choice but to modify their plans to incorporate part of the old North Stand into the new stadium. Nicknamed Glanmor's Gap by supporters, after the WRU's Secretary, it remains in place to this day,

a testament to the sometimes fraught relationship between the governing body and the clubs in the professional era. Despite this, the continuing pace of change on site was impressive. Over 40,000 tons of concrete and 4,000 tons of steel reinforcement were brought in. The soft alluvial soils along the river meant foundation piles had to be driven in to a depth of 1,350 feet (412 metres) to prevent subsidence.

As work progressed on the stadium itself in Cardiff, its roof was under construction some distance from Wales in Pordenone, northern Italy, at the factories of Cimolai Costruzioni Metalliche. As with Laings, they had been involved in another huge Welsh building project which involved steel,

the second Severn Crossing. The steel for the roof was produced in Wales and then shipped to Italy for fabrication. The completed sections were then shipped back to Cardiff docks and brought into the city. Not all of it made the return journey successfully, as during a violent storm in the Bay of Biscay, one section was lost overboard and a replacement had to be shipped later. Once unloaded at the docks, the huge roof sections had to be carefully manoeuvred through the city at night to avoid disruption, and then lifted by Europe's largest crane onto massive temporary steel support towers.

By the spring of 1999 work was continuing around the clock, but doubts were being expressed that the project would not be finished on time. A riverside walkway was added outside the West Stand but with so little room between the Taff and the stadium, it had to be designed so that it overhung the river. When completed it gave the citizens of Cardiff access to that section of the river bank for the first time in decades. Despite the organisers of the Rugby World Cup making contingency plans to hold the tournament elsewhere in case of an overrun on the build, Glanmor Griffiths rebuffed all suggestions that the stadium would not be ready. Such was the WRU's confidence that work was temporarily halted in June for the 7,412 pallets that made up the pitch to be brought into the stadium (which was still a building site), to host its first match. The world champions and Wales's traditional nemesis, South

72 of 500

GRAND SLAM
WRU
CYMRU
WINNERS 2005

BRAINS

A special limited edition jersey was produced to celebrate the 2005 Grand Slam. This one bears the signatures of the first Welsh team to win a "Slam" since 1978.

Africa, were invited to be the first opponents on 26 June 1999. A lucky 27,000 ticket holders were admitted to the completed sections to make history as the Millennium Stadium's first crowd. They also got to watch history too as Wales, coached by New Zealander Graham Henry, defeated the South Africans for the first time 29–19, with Mark Taylor (Swansea) scoring the new ground's first try, for which he received a commemorative gold ring. Almost as soon as the game ended and the crowd headed off to celebrate, much of the pitch was removed and work resumed.

There followed a frantic few months as work neared completion and Wales played a series of World Cup warm-up games which were as much a rehearsal for the stadium and its staff as they were for the team. By late September, just thirty months since the last game at the National Stadium, the Millennium Stadium had taken its place. Despite the doubters, the WRU and its contractors had delivered the largest roofed stadium in Europe and arguably the world's finest rugby stadium in the heart of the Welsh capital. In spite of the time pressure and rapid pace of work, not one workman was seriously injured during construction. With a justifiable sense of pride Wales could now welcome the rugby world to the magnificent new incarnation of Cardiff Arms Park.

The Rugby World Cup kicked off on the 1 October with Wales defeating Argentina 23–18 in a tense game. For the next five weeks, the Millennium Stadium was the focus of the sporting

Australian Captain John Eales (centre) surrounded by his World Cup winning team of 1999. Eales was nicknamed "nobody" by his team mates because as they said, "Nobody's perfect".

world. Wales progressed to the quarter finals before being defeated by the eventual winners Australia. Led by John Eales, the Australians went on to beat France 35–12 in the final and become the first country to win the Rugby World Cup twice. The new stadium, with its magnificent intense atmosphere and superb views of the pitch, became the real star of the show. Over half a million people had attended the games and the global television audience topped three billion in 147 countries. Things had moved a long way since the £50 grandstand of 1881.

One of the key features of the Millennium Stadium is its versatility in hosting different events. The removable pitch, retractable roof and central location made it a sought-after venue for concerts and much more. This began almost as soon as the Rugby World Cup had ended with Wales's leading rock band, the Manic Street Preachers, playing a Millennium Eve gig to 70,000 fans in the world's largest indoor concert. Just days later, a very different Welsh musical experience was hosted at Welsh rugby's new home, when 60,000 worshippers attended a hymn and choral concert for the BBC's *Songs of Praise* programme in the world's largest televised religious service.

In 2000, championship rugby returned from its Wembley exile, but it was no longer the Five Nations, which had ended in 1999 with Wales's dramatic 32–31 victory over England at Wembley. Italy had now joined to create the Six Nations Championship and so the banks of the Taff experienced its largest Roman invasion for 2,000 years, as legions of Italian rugby supporters headed to Cardiff.

The connection with Wembley, created by Wales's period in exile, did not end with the return of the national side to Cardiff. Inspired by the work at the Arms Park, the decision was taken that the famous but ageing ground in London needed redevelopment and, as a result, its events need to be rehoused, including the FA Cup, League Cup, Play-Offs and Rugby League Challenge Cup. The choice of a temporary venue was obvious and so, from 2001, the Millennium Stadium became the centre of English football and rugby league as well as Welsh rugby. Just few years before the prospect of rugby league on the Arms Park would have been unthinkable but with the advent of professional rugby union, the century of division between the two rugby codes had eased. In the first football final at the Millennium Stadium, Liverpool defeated Arsenal 2–1 to win the first FA Cup not played on English soil. Delays in the Wembley project meant the finals kept returning to Cardiff for six years, with some of the world's most famous clubs appearing, including Manchester United, Spurs and Chelsea amongst them. The new stadium was

The 125th FA Cup Final in 2006 saw Liverpool defeat West Ham in the greatest final of the modern era. It was the last of six FA Cup Finals to be held at the ground, the first was also one by Liverpool who defeated Arsenal in 2001. Between 2001 and 2007 over 40 English domestic football finals were held at the home of Welsh rugby.

rapidly able to establish its reputation as a world class venue and became known all over the globe, not just in the rugby playing nations.

More and more sports were added to the stadium's CV including cricket (back at the ground for the first time since Glamorgan's departure in 1966), netball, show-jumping, petanque and the ground also became the finishing line for the Cardiff Marathon. Boxing made a return in 2006, but it was in 2007 that the stadium hosted its most memorable bouts as Welsh legend and world super-middle-weight champion Joe Calzaghe fought twice at the Millennium Stadium. The second bout against Mikkel Kessler unified the WBO, WBA and WBC titles. Motor sports also

Supporters' headgear has moved on from the bowlers and flat caps of a century before. Not the best development if you have the seats behind them, mind you.

beat a path to the stadium with regular British Speedway Grand Prix, motocross, Monster Trucks and, in 2005, the roof was closed to stage the World Rally Championship's first ever indoor stage during the Wales Rally GB.

The Millennium Stadium also picked up where

the National Stadium had begun, by establishing itself firmly on the rock concert circuit. Its compact design, closing roof and proximity to the city centre's amenities made it one of the best concert stadiums anywhere in the world. Following on from the Manic Street Preachers, the list of bands

Being taken to your first international is a day to remember for any youngster and not a bad day for mums and dads either.

areas devastated by the Indian Ocean tsunami. Over twenty acts, headlined by Eric Clapton, played a seven-hour concert to 60,000 people and raised almost £2 million. The Millennium Stadium was a fitting venue for the concert, standing as it does on land engulfed by the sea but 400 years earlier, during Britain's worst flood disaster in 1607. These concerts, as well as other events like conferences, banquets, a funfair, a giant casino and New Year's Eve parties all became part of the new ground's story (not always to the delight of the purists), but with rugby now a professional game the WRU's major asset had to be put to work to raise money for the running costs of the Welsh game. The income the stadium generates has become crucial to rugby but also to the wider economy of both Cardiff and Wales. In its first decade the Millennium Stadium contributed over a billion pounds to the Welsh economy.

International football adapted quickly to the new ground with frequent sell-out games as the Welsh side came agonisingly close to qualifying for the 2004 European Championships before falling to Russia in a play-off. During the campaign under manager Mark Hughes the side did produce one of the great nights in Welsh football history however, when Wales defeated Italy 2–1 with goals from Simon Davies and Craig Bellamy. There was Welsh success at the ground at domestic level also, when both Swansea and Wrexham won the FA Trophy, and there was home-town success for Cardiff City

has included U2, The Rolling Stones, Bruce Springsteen, Madonna, Oasis, Red Hot Chili Peppers, Take That, the Foo Fighters, Tina Turner, Bon Jovi, the Stereophonics and many more. A very unusual concert took place on 22 January 2005: the Tsunami Relief Concert raised funds for

Henson dumping O'Driscoll.

The intensity of a Six Nations game in Cardiff on the face of Wales's record try scorer Shane Williams as he celebrates his decisive score in the Grand Slam win over France in 2008.

when they gained promotion to the Championship in a nail-biting 1–0 play-off final win over Queens Park Rangers.

It was rugby however that remained at the heart of the new ground's life, just as it had done at all the previous grounds on the site over the preceding century and a quarter. But, the opening decade of the new millennium must rank as one of the most tempestuous in the Welsh game's history. Ironically, the enormous financial strain of building the new stadium contributed to this, along with the financial cost of the professional game. Relationships between the clubs and the WRU deteriorated and international success remained elusive.

In 2003, the WRU introduced 'regional rugby' in the biggest shake up of the domestic game since the Union's formation. The need for a reorganisation to fewer professional sides was not disputed by anyone, but the manner in which it was carried out left a great deal to be desired and seemed to create as many problems as it solved. Five 'new' regional sides were created, although some were distinctly less regional than others with Cardiff and Llanelli demanding and getting the right not to merge with other clubs. Apart from the addition of the rather bland 'Blues' to Cardiff and 'Scarlets' (which had been their nickname for a century) to Llanelli they carried on largely as before. Elsewhere the situation became

The palletised pitch at the Millennium Stadium Cardiff Arms Park allows the venue to host a wider variety of events than any previous stadium on this site. This brings valuable revenue to the WRU and local economy. In its first decade the new stadium brought over a billion pounds into the local economy.

more complicated and increasingly unworkable. At Newport a disastrous attempt at merger with Ebbw Vale ended in dispute. The WRU's solution to call the side Gwent Dragons and unwisely ignore the wishes of the large Newport support base to include their club's name, predictably ended in turmoil as fans boycotted the side. Ebbw Vale pulled out and the Newport name was rapidly put back in to prevent disaster. Swansea and Neath merged to form the Ospreys and for a time this went relatively smoothly, but before long, disputes arose and Neath's involvement became increasingly remote. Most controversially was the fate of the fifth side, the Celtic Warriors, which was a merger between Bridgend and Pontypridd. After a season of poor crowds the WRU disbanded the side, creating the four sides they had initially wanted, but it was an action which angered many rugby supporters in the area. The problem the Union faced was that for its entire history Welsh rugby's strength had been the fierce and passionate club rivalries which had inspired players and supporters. Attempting to replace this with something completely new was always going to be problematic and to have attempted to introduce a system which treated clubs differently was doomed. Despite official talk of regions and the Welsh media's rather forced, clumsy use of new nicknames like Dragons and Blues in place Newport or Cardiff, the reality was increasingly that the four new 'regions' very closely resembled the traditional 'Big Four' of Cardiff, Newport, Swansea and Llanelli which had been the cornerstones of the domestic game. The club tradition was too deeply ingrained to be swept away and the wisdom of even trying was questionable at best. Once their initial novelty had worn off, the peculiarly bland identities of the regional sides increasingly resembled Welsh rugby's equivalent of the 1960s tower blocks;

far more admired by their architects than by the public they were intended for.

At international level events were every bit as dramatic. Wales had employed two New Zealand coaches, Graham Henry and Steve Hansen, who had done much to restore Wales's standing, but by 2004 both had returned to New Zealand. The WRU appointed Mike Ruddock, coach of the Newport Gwent Dragons, as their new man. This came as a shock to many in Wales, not least the Newport Gwent Dragons, as Ruddock had not applied for the job. However, once the controversy had died down Wales produced a promising display against New Zealand before narrowly losing 25–26 in November 2004. There was some optimism about the 2005 Six Nations Championship but nobody expected what was about to unfold. The opening game, a tense victory over England 11–9 was settled by a single Shane Williams (Neath, Ospreys) try and a late Gavin Henson (Swansea, Ospreys, Cardiff Blues) penalty. In the next three games, all away from home, the Welsh side revealed an attacking threat which delighted supporters and surprised their opponents as Italy, France and Scotland were beaten. Everything now depended on the final game against Ireland at the Millennium Stadium on 19 March 2005. Wales had gone through a barren twenty-seven year wait for a Grand Slam and in the week leading up to the match it became virtually the only topic of conversation across the country. On the day of

the match a huge crowd of a quarter of a million people descended on Cardiff. Every bar, pub and club was packed while a giant screen was erected outside City Hall for 30,000 to watch in the sunshine. Around 74,500 holders of the most prized tickets in a generation (2.5 per cent of the Welsh population) packed the Millennium Stadium as the tension grew. A pulsating game in an unforgettable atmosphere saw Wales triumph 32–20 with tries by Gethin Jenkins (Pontypridd, Celtic Warriors, Cardiff Blues) and Kevin Morgan (Pontypridd, Celtic Warriors, Newport Gwent Dragons). The sense of relief, as much as celebration, that the wait was over will never be forgotten by anyone who was there or watching outside. As the BBC's Brian Moore famously remarked, the grandstand was 'literally shaking' as the final whistle sounded.

The Welsh resurgence on the field wasn't to last however as the roller coaster decade took a downward turn. Amid rumours of dressing room unrest Mike Ruddock suddenly resigned in 2006. The 2007 Rugby World Cup was one Wales would rather forget, as they were eliminated at the pool stage after a defeat by Fiji in Nantes. Wales's coach Gareth Jenkins was replaced by Warren Gatland (a New Zealander who had coached Ireland and Wasps) and his assistant Shaun Edwards (the former rugby league star). Then in another dramatic change of fortune, Wales put their humiliation of a few months earlier behind them and won the 2008 Six Nations, claiming a tenth Grand Slam. Hard-fought away wins in England and Ireland and home victories over Italy and Scotland meant everything depended on the visit of France to the Millennium Stadium. With the roof closed to keep out the rain, the game was played in an intense atmosphere and was deadlocked for an hour, when a French mistake was pounced upon by Shane Williams who sped away to score under the posts. Martyn Williams (Pontypridd, Cardiff, Cardiff Blues) scored another try late on to seal the win and claim the first Grand Slam ever won indoors.

In 2011, the WRU celebrated its 130th anniversary. Throughout this long period the sporting events which have taken place on the few acres of land they own beside the river Taff have often been the intense focus of the people of Wales and, at times of great success especially, have almost helped to define the nation itself. It says a great deal that Wales has its rugby stadium right at the heart of its capital city. Despite many suggestions and threats to remove it somewhere else, it remains as a great reminder of the significance and importance the people of Wales give to their national side. In a typically busy year, the Millennium Stadium Cardiff Arms Park hosted Six Nations games, rugby league matches, a Welsh football international, the Heineken European Cup Final, rock concerts, a celebration match with the Barbarians and warm-up games before the 2011 Rugby World Cup in New Zealand. In 2012, the stadium will also have the honour of hosting the first event of the Olympic Games with a series of football matches.

The magnificent ground has become an icon of its city and country, a vital part of the local economy and a source of pride to the people of Wales. The modern stadium and the variety and scale of the events it hosts may seem a world away from the original 1881 grandstand built 130 years ago for £50 (less than the price of a match ticket today), but they are both chapters in the same continuing story, the story of Cardiff Arms Park, the heart of a rugby nation.

Postscript

At the time of writing the futures of both the iconic Arms Park name and a significant part of the site are uncertain. The Cardiff club ground at the northern end of the Arms Park, the part which still bears the famous name, has recently been the subject of speculation over its continuation as a sporting venue. In 2009 Cardiff's first team, re-branded as the Cardiff Blues, decamped to the newly built Cardiff City Stadium, home of Cardiff City Football Club, at Leckwith on the city's western outskirts. The move proved deeply unpopular with many supporters who preferred the familiar, more close-knit atmosphere of a rugby ground and bitterly regretted the end of their long association with their famous home. The loss of the unrivalled central location was another source of regret for many but it is precisely this central location which has brought the pressure for development, not for the first time in the Arms Park's history. This time however the financial stresses of professional rugby made the threat to the ground's sporting future from potential development seem very serious, and unlike in the past, there will be no Marquess of Bute stepping in to secure the ground's sporting usage. Cardiff RFC's semi-professional side (affectionately known as the 'Rags' by supporters) continue to play at the Arms Park for the time being, but if Cardiff Athletic Club ever do sell up and relocate then the northern section of the Arms Park could disappear for ever beneath the foundations of a conference centre or apartments. However, such is the strength of feeling amongst Cardiff supporters in favour of the club's first team ending their unwanted exile, a return may yet become a welcome reality and the sporting future of that part of the Arms Park could be secured.

Sport will continue on the southern section of the site however, as it plays host to the WRU's magnificent Millennium Stadium, the home of Welsh international matches and so much more. Sadly, the present WRU seem increasingly reluctant to use the most famous address in Wales. What was previously known as the Millennium Stadium, Cardiff Arms Park is now simply 'Millennium Stadium' with the historic title reduced to somewhat token usage as the name of a function room and a shop on Westgate Street. A sad fate for a name which has inspired and enthused generations of Welsh people, has

Sign of the times. In 2009 Cardiff's professional side, branded Cardiff Blues in 2003, quit the Arms Park to play at the Cardiff City Stadium on the outskirts of the city. The controversial move was unpopular with many supporters who wanted a return to their iconic home. With crowds at the new venue dwindling badly, Cardiff Blues returned to the Arms Park in February 2012 for a sell-out match with Irish side Connacht and the prospect of further matches at the famous ground to follow.

The sign below advertises a second tier game between Cardiff RFC and Llanelli RFC, two of Welsh rugby's historic names. Llanelli's professional side, the Scarlets (formerly the Llanelli Scarlets) are a continuation of the 'pre-regional' Llanelli RFC side, who were known as the Scarlets, while Llanelli RFC continue as the club's second team but are not known as the Scarlets. Welcome to Wales.

Quite what the great Gwyn Nicholls, whose elegant memorial gates lead into Cardiff's section of the Arms Park, would make of all this is open to conjecture.

Towering over everything is a mast of the Millennium Stadium, the WRU's section of the Arms Park.

welcomed the world to Wales and taken Wales to the world. It's not the first time attempts have been made to elbow out the famous name. Back in the early 1980s the use of 'National Ground' and 'National Stadium' were introduced prompting Cardiff, Wales and Lions great Gerald Davies to write an article in the WRU's centenary gala programme entitled 'It Will Always Be The Arms Park.' In it Davies summed up what many Welsh people felt about adopting a new name: 'The very sound of it lacks warmth, cold and impersonal like a government department acting to nationalise a successful enterprise. It is bland and unevocative, and curiously anonymous and not in keeping at all with a country which seeks identity and where people are characteristically parochial, sharp and colourful, aware of the image and the undying tradition.' Fortunately 'Cardiff Arms Park' was attached to the new name back then and hopefully will be reinstated in it's proper place today. Millennium Stadium, Cardiff Arms Park says so much more than the rather bland Millennium Stadium.

Unfortunately if it is to be quietly dropped from the name of Welsh rugby's citadel this would be in keeping with how the heritage of Welsh rugby is currently preserved and presented, or more accurately, how it isn't. Despite the passion the game inspires and the major role it has played in popular culture for generations there is no museum of Welsh rugby, nowhere for the people of Wales and visitors from around the world to explore and celebrate the unique bond between the nation and the game. Many Welsh clubs do a thorough job of recording and displaying their individual heritage but the history of the national game as a whole is sadly neglected. The WRU's own collection of items from their history lies locked deep down inside the Millennium Stadium, while the more diligent work many private collectors do in preserving the game's heritage remains by its nature private and out of reach to most people. This presents a stark contrast to the situation across the border in England where the Rugby Football Union are able to boast a very fine museum, attracting thousand of visitors, to their Twickenham home. Given the game's far greater role in Welsh popular culture, its status as the 'national game' and its importance in gaining international attention for Wales, it is a great shame that there is no equivalent venue telling the unique story of Welsh rugby at the WRU's headquarters in the heart of the capital. It is hoped the WRU will one day create such a facility to show this rich heritage, and there could be no more fitting address for this than Cardiff Arms Park.

Bibliography

Acknowledgements

Terry Breverton, *The Book of Welsh Pirates and Buccaneers* (Cowbridge, 2003)

John Davies, *Cardiff: A Pocket Guide* (Cardiff, 2002)

John Davies, *Cardiff and the Marquesses of Bute* (University of Wales Press)

Duncan Gardiner and Alan Evans, *Cardiff Rugby Football Club 1876–1939*, The History Press Ltd

Steve Lewis, *Newport Rugby Football Club*, Vols 1 and 2 (Stroud, 1999)

Dennis Morgan, *Discovering Cardiff's Past* (Llandysul, 1995)

Dennis Morgan, *The Cardiff Story* (Tonypandy, 2001)

Kenneth O Morgan, *Re-birth of a Nation. Wales 1880–1980* (Oxford, 1981)

David Parry Jones (ed.), *Taff's Acre. A History and Celebration of Cardiff Arms Park* (London, 1984)

Clive Rowlands (ed.) *Giants of Post-War Welsh Rugby* (Swansea, 1990)

David Smith and Gareth Williams, Fields of Praise. *The Official History of the Welsh Rugby Union 1881–1981* (Cardiff, 1980)

Graham Smith, *Smuggling in the Bristol Channel: 1700–1850* (Newbury, 1989)

Wynford Vaughan-Thomas, *Wales: A History* (London, 1985)

The authors and publishers gratefully thank the following for permission granted for the use of photographic material and original artwork in this book:

Cardiff Athletic Club; Cardiff RFC, Brian Bennett; Cardiff Castle, Matthew Williams; Timothy Auty Collection; Dai Richards, Rugby Relics; Cardiff Library; Philip J Grant; Newport RFC; Roger Bowles; Media Wales; Getty Images; Andrew Hignell, Glamorgan County Cricket Club; The Institute of Engineers; The Mountstuart Estate; The WRU Collection; The Glamorgan Archive; Ian Soulsby; Construction Photography, Adrian Greeman; Emyr Young; Bob Luxford, New Zealand Rugby Museum; The Glamorgan Archive.

Thanks also to the following:

Rupert Moon; Howard Evans; Ray Ruddick; Carolyn Hitt; Pat Thompson, Cardiff County Council; Gareth Harvey; John Hood; The Rugby Memorabilia Society; special thanks to Kempton Rees of Darwin Gray Solicitors.

The Arms Park is just one of a whole range
of publications from Y Lolfa. For a full list of
books currently in print, send now for your
free copy of our new full-colour catalogue.
Or simply surf into our website

www.ylolfa.com

for secure on-line ordering.

TALYBONT CEREDIGION CYMRU SY24 5HE
e-mail ylolfa@ylolfa.com
website www.ylolfa.com
phone (01970) 832 304
fax 832 782